DOGS ARE FROM NEPTUNE

Candid answers to urgent questions about aggression
and other aspects of dog behavior

Jean Donaldson

Lasar Multimedia Productions

Dogs Are From Neptune
By Jean Donaldson

Published in Canada by:

Lasar Multimedia Productions Inc.
1250 René-Lévesque Blvd. W., Suite 2200
Montreal, Quebec H3B 4W8
(514) 989-3711

http://www.lasardogs.com

pictured on cover : Oakcroft's Princess Katana (the Vilderbeest)
and Meggie (El Diablo)

ISBN 0-9684207-1-0

For Meggie

ACKNOWLEDGEMENTS

I would like to express thanks and acknowledgement to the following:

First and foremost, to James Klein, for being the driving force and an awe-inspiring genius in a dizzying array of endeavors, and to Alichan Hajjar, for always being in my corner, putting up with me and being my rock

Carolyn Clark, for believing in my ideas, without falter, since day one

Martin Coles, for coming up with such stunning cover art

Ian Dunbar, the one and only, for showing us all how to train dogs

Susan Gillett, for never failing to deliver, be it timely advice, encouragement or a pair of hands

Delva Howell, for supplying her dog for the photo shoot, for the example of her awesome dog training talent, and for taking the time so often to call and say "good answer this week!"

Judy Miller, for being able to so brilliantly clean up my writing without ever once bruising my feelings

Kathy Pickel, for teaching me so much about people, for innumerable instances of pitching in and contributing above and beyond the call, and for talking me off cliffs on more than one occasion

Tony Stalls, for being an intelligent, game and yet tactful sounding-board and for endless unwavering personal support

And to the people who wrote in to the website with such thought-provoking questions about their dogs

Table of Contents

Behavior Problems

Obedience Problems

Fear & Anxiety

Subject Index   161

INTRODUCTION

When we started the "Question of the Week" feature on our website, I expected occasional submissions of straightforward questions that I would answer in a paragraph or two. It would be like a newspaper personal advice column.

The questions were light years ahead of my feeble expectation and poured in like an avalanche. I found myself drafting, researching, agonizing and re-drafting to come up with the answers warranted by these questions so rich in complexity, issues and nuance.

The book is divided into six sections. The first three deal with aggression. This was by far the most frequently submitted topic and, to me, the least well handled by both dog owners and dog professionals.

The second half of the book is devoted to a sampling of questions on behavior, obedience and anxiety-related problems. Some of these questions opened up interesting side avenues to explore.

In most cases, certain identifying features have been changed to protect anonymity. Aside from this and standard editing for length and clarity, the questions remain as they were originally presented.

I am continually impressed by the sophistication and sincerity some owners bring to their tireless efforts at understanding their dog companions and helping them to fit into our world. They are, for dog trainers everywhere, a powerful antidote to owners at the other end of the spectrum.

Jean Donaldson
October 14, 1998

AGGRESSION TOWARDS STRANGERS

Undersocialized to Men

I have just acquired a three year old newly neutered Great Dane, from a loving female breeder. We have had him two weeks. Reggie is a former champion and therapy dog. He is docile and loving, and has coped beautifully with everything so far, except men. He has bitten my eighteen-year-old son on the nose and growls at him or my husband if they appear suddenly. He is either my or my daughter's shadow. He loves to come in the car, and males outside of the home do not seem to be a problem. When a male friend comes to the house there is much noise and growling. Females are accepted quickly.

Yesterday, a friend of my son rode home with us in the van. When he entered the car Reggie growled, trembled and appeared very menacing. After about 5 minutes he stopped trembling and the thirty-minute ride went without incident.

We are somewhat alarmed. Is there anything we can do?

Yes, you ought to be able to gradually improve Reggie's behavior towards men. In your favor is a probably well executed overall socialization he got as a show dog and therapy dog. This provides a foot in the door for work on the specific problem you have. As an analogy, imagine an overall physically fit person who has done lots of sports. This person will have an edge learning tennis as compared to another rank novice who is relatively unfit and has never learned other sports. Reggie has had numerous times in his show and therapy career, we hope, the experience of being a little iffy about something, getting exposed to it over and over and then becoming more comfortable. His habituation "muscle" has had some development, in other words. This doesn't mean Reggie is not undersocialized to men - he obviously is, and socialization is quite specific in dogs - but he is a better candidate for remedial work, all other things being equal, than a dog of his age who had feeble overall socialization. Kind of a bad news, good news thing.

I have reservations about men outside the house not being a problem and I would caution you to not be too cavalier in your handling of him outdoors. The problem may be masked. The specific case of men on the street has probably come to predict extreme low probability of contact or over-proximity. The combination of some habituation to this scenario and its low predictiveness of scarier levels of interaction make for what seems so puzzling: why hate men in the house and accept them outside? Before presuming territoriality, rule out undersocialization.

Are men on the street, for instance, able to pat him? If he spooks when there is direct interaction or physical contact, then this would ice it. If he doesn't, it would point to some territorial defense component or else a superstitious or learned element to his fear in the house or the car. If it turns out he does spook when men try to pat him outside, add outdoor exercises to your program.

Here's what you can do: recognize that Reggie's behavior is an emotional reaction and not a volitional behavior. Rewards and punishments will only scratch the surface. What *will* get at the root is to deliberately condition a competing emotional response with the presence of, proximity of and, eventually, contact with men as the sole predictor. The best way to maximize this effect is to reserve his favorite things in the world for when mane are around. This might be a game or an out-of-this world treat he never, ever gets otherwise. It should be potent and coveted and it should appear when men are on the scene and disappear when men disappear. It should happen over and over so that a strong trend emerges. It also means that *regardless of his behavior*, the good thing should happen to him when men are around.

This flies in the face of operant theory but remember, the main thing you are going for is a classical conditioning effect, i.e. a stimulus (men) to stimulus (favorite game/goody) connection and not an operant contingency (this behavior produces X consequence). Don't fret too much about the latter - he will get the game or goody when men are around and sometimes he will be growling, sometimes he will be cocking his head at you, sometimes he will be sniffing them at a distance etc. etc. No one behavior will get a strong conditioning history - the ONE thing that predicts the game/goody bar opening is that men are around. His behavior is irrelevant.

Now, that said, we don't want him rehearsing his probably self-reinforcing aggressive behavior ("Get away from me! GRRRRR!!! Phew! They're gone! See how well it works...") because this definitely dents the cause, so **you** will manipulate the intensity of the men, especially early on. He won't be in the mood to play or eat if the scary men are too intensely presented anyway.

The best way to manipulate their intensity is to use distance. Keep them far enough away, so that he *notices* them and is a bit edgy but not having a full-blown fear reaction. You could also use the men's posture - oblique/ignoring ones that predict low likelihood of approach or contact - or the overall context - ones that predict low likelihood of approach or contact, such as the street - to make it easy at first. If possible, avoid ever forcing men on him at levels that elicit a full-blown spooking reaction (growling etc.). While you may get significant changes within weeks, it is more likely that big changes will take months.

Eventually you will want to cover lots of bases location-wise and other variable-wise to make sure you haven't left any holes unplugged. But this is done gradually as is any bump up in level of difficulty. Start off conservatively.

It is as important that the "bar" closes when men go away as it is that it opens when they appear. If the good stuff happens in other contexts it dilutes the effect. The game or goodies need not come *from* the men, but they must occur in their presence. It can come from you: "Reggie, look! Yippee! Dad's in the room! The bar is OPEN!!!" (proceed to initiate game or give coveted treat)..."Oh dear, he's left, bar closed" (end game, stop treat flow, ignore dog). It also sure wouldn't hurt to have your son and husband become the principal "good guys" in the household. Any good news for Reggie

DOGS ARE FROM NEPTUNE

(cookie time, play ball time, walk time etc.) could come from them. The boys in the house need the currency more than you do. Also, any bad guy stuff should come from the women (nail clipping if he dislikes it, reprimanding if there is to be any etc.).

Construct a hit list. Do multiple trials of each (singles are almost worthless). For instance, do your son's friend getting in and out of the van over and over, many times in a row, opening and closing the bar in a pointed fashion so the connection is clear: no male kid, no open bar (Reggie: "wow, I wish they would bring that 18-year old guy back..."). Remember, you're trying to establish a trend. Give him lots of data. Here are a few suggestions for your hit list:

- Dad in or out of room
- Son in or out of room
- Dad in close proximity/approach
- Son in close proximity/approach
- Dad - physical contact (gradually increasing in invasiveness or duration)
- Son - physical contact (ditto)
- Dad - sudden appearance or movement
- Son - sudden appearance or movement
- Dad - bizarre behavior
- Son - bizarre behavior
- Dad - physical startle (unexpected contact)
- Son - physical startle
- Strange male entering house - hit all age ranges, physical types and anything else you note he notices (some dogs care about voice/facial hair etc. etc. whereas some dogs don't register this in a big way)
- Strange male in house approaching dog
- Strange male riding in van with dog
- Strange male touching dog while in van
- Strange male on street approaching dog
- Strange male on street making sudden movement or appearance
- Any situation you encounter where he reacts badly: reconstruct it later with more distance and multiple trials (see a spook

AGGRESSION TOWARDS STRANGERS

reaction as information: "here is another piece of the puzzle I can tackle!")

Many of the exercises are hierarchical: the dad and son stuff at the beginning get progressively more difficult. For these, only move on to a more difficult level when he's really, really comfortable, even actively **happy** about the level you're already on (Reggie: "yippee! 18-year-old son is going to touch me! BAR OPEN!!!!!"). Others are just bases to cover. You can always break down something he's having more difficulty with. Don't agonize too much about pace of improvement. Chip away at the problem whenever knocks: have bait always on you just in case. With a narrow, well-defined problem like this, you have the luxury of working opportunistically.

Dogs like Great Danes, who are good guard dogs, have a low threshold for spooking at sudden environmental contrast (SEC). To get a feel for SEC, imagine a dog that can walk down a busy street past scores of people and be very relaxed. The same dog walking down the same street on another day when the street is empty spooks if one person suddenly appears from around the corner. It may not be that person, or people that is the problem so much as the abrupt contrast. At the other extreme, there are dogs (e.g. many hounds) whose reactivity is so low that they barely notice events that would spook a Dane or GSD into outer space, not to mention startling you or me into cardiac arrest.

SEC, physical startle or bizarre behavior are things Reggie may have issues about quite apart from his issues with men. This goes for many dogs, by the way. They are important bases to cover. Pave the way with the female members of the household first before stacking up risk factors (i.e. combining men with startle...).

I wish there were a quick fix for this. It's a fascinating process, however, and an opportunity to watch classical conditioning in action in the real world. If you're struggling with the nuts and bolts, get in touch with the Animal Behavior Society or APDT (1-800-PET-DOGS).

DOGS ARE FROM NEPTUNE

Severely Unsocialized Dog in Group Class

I instruct Pet Dog Classes and I have a six month-old Bouvier in one class that is so fear-aggressive that he doesn't just bark but lunges, screeching, whenever there is any movement near him. The owner did not socialize him as a puppy. I have tried throwing treats on the floor and he has finally started picking them up, especially if I am in a sideways, passive position. I have almost gotten to the point of being able to walk up to a chair near him and sit sideways. He usually throws himself toward me, displaying, but now has started sniffing a bit.

He is a very scary dog and upsets the other dogs in the class. Last week the owner was sick and didn't attend. The other students mentioned how quiet the class was, how they could hear my instruction and some mentioned that the whole thing was upsetting their dogs. This week when the owner returned to class I sat next to Archie and again it was the same reaction. I told her that his behavior is very upsetting to the rest of the class and suggested that we do some private lessons to first get him used to me and then to start to socialize him slowly. I really felt badly but she understood and left the class. Do you have any suggestions? I know that the steps have to be baby steps; I don't want to push too hard but I don't want the owner to give up.

Your question raises a couple of different issues: one is how to address remedial socialization and the other is the kind of dogs we should be screening out of group obedience classes.

Socializing a six-month-old Bouvier who missed the boat as a puppy is going to take patience (i.e. months rather than days). You're absolutely right that part of the worry here is that the owner will give up. The long-winded, deferred gratification training endeavors - socialization, aggression, fear, and anxiety - are at highest risk for the fizzling out brand owner non-compliance. So, she needs support: a) clear instructions and a prognosis: what to expect regarding pace of progress and final result and b) handholding and cheerleading. It's no fun living with a dog like this.

6

AGGRESSION TOWARDS STRANGERS

To make the dog gradually more comfortable around strangers (and other specific triggers like movement, approach, novelty etc.), you have two ways to go: opportunistically or an all-out assault. The former means making the most of the opportunities that come down the pike in the normal course of the dog's life. Any visitors to the house, for instance, must abide by a regime that at the very least does not exacerbate the dog's fearfulness and hopefully will inch the dog in the right direction.

This means sufficient distance (baby-gates if the dog is a displayer, freedom to flee if the dog is a fleer) so the dog does not feel threatened, and **religious** treat flow while the visitors are present. The owner needs to also protect the dog from people coming on too strong on the street, which would blow your hard-won baby steps out of the water - the "it's okay, I know how to approach dogs..." types can wreck a carefully orchestrated socialization effort. You have an excellent instinct for pace from what you've described. To supplement your efforts to befriend him, the owner can carry treats or a favorite toy on all walks and supply this after every person encounter. People = good stuff.

Although with this style of socialization the odds are poor at making significant gains in a case like Archie's, the likelihood of owner compliance is high. It's easy enough to do and may prevent further downhill slide and even promote gains over the long haul. It's better than nothing. But, to **really** make a dent, an all-out assault is the way to go. This means *relentless daily exposure* to social stimuli at a level the dog can tolerate, with a gradual increase in intensity as the dog improves. I'm more and more convinced that relentless daily exposure is the key.

Put it this way: the frequency and intensity of spooky dogs increases as proximity to an urban center increases. For instance, I live in the middle of a large city with two herding dogs, one of whom comes from a spooky line (close to 100% "fear biters" on the mother's side - world class stupid shopping on my part, but that's beyond the scope here). And yet, she is an unflappable rock in

DOGS ARE FROM NEPTUNE

spite of the fact that I make no active effort at maintaining her level of socialization. Why is this?

What *does* happen is that every time the dogs go for a pee, they encounter novel people, sights and sounds. Every single time. Scores of new people a day. All sizes, shapes and demographics patting them, screeching dog phobics refusing to ride the elevator with them, skateboards, bikes, strollers, drunken university students, moving vans, wheelchairs, emergencies, football fans with beer hats, couriers, homeless people dancing around talking to themselves, film crews - and this is just short trips to the bathroom. Long walks and exercise trips are more stimulating. They have not only seen it all: they continue to see it all every day.

I plan to move to suburbia in the next couple of years. My prediction is that my dogs will gradually spook over after this happens. The effect will be somewhat minor after a lifetime downtown but I would bet money it occurs. Suburban dog syndrome. What do dogs in suburbia see on walks? Do they even get walks or mainly see the yard? What's the daily quotient of novel stimuli? What about dogs in DEEP suburbia? What about "the country?" Compare this to the picture of downtown: automatic, even if unintentional, assault-style socialization. Ship this Bouv to live in Manhattan for a couple of years and watch what happens. This is a big lesson for us working with intractable socialization cases.

The rub is this: what kind of owner, if they don't have default daily access to this kind of environment, is going to seek it out in order to improve their dog's degree of socialization? And keep up the constant pressure to avoid regression? Very few. It's not realistic. So the question becomes: what is the minimum amount and intensity to make and maintain decent gains? And can it be made do-able for the owner? No one knows the precise answer to this question. I suspect the answer is different in every case. It's safe to say the more volume and variety the better. Long walks in public places, regular traffic through the house and dog-trade "vacations" with more urban-dwelling friends are possible avenues to beef up the effort.

AGGRESSION TOWARDS STRANGERS

The other issue, about screening dogs before acceptance into group courses, is also important. Most schools have policies to filter severely fearful and aggressive adolescent and adult dogs into private training for both the sake of the dog and the other students who are there to learn obedience. The level of stimulation in a class is too high for these dogs initially, though many would benefit from a reward-oriented obedience class after working up to that level privately. This screening is easily done over the phone on initial client contact with a couple of standardized questions: "Does he like strangers?" and "How is he with other dogs?" Explore further if the owner replies with anything other than "loves."

The gray area cases, the mild-to-moderates, can often go either way. Sometimes, with the owner's informed consent up front, they can be put in a group class on spec. If, by, say, week 3, there is not substantial gain and/or they are excessively disruptive (judgment calls I realize), switch to plan B: privates. The curriculum for the private lessons can be divided between obedience and remedial socialization. Most instructors would say you made the right call with the Bouvier, by a long shot. He's not ready for class yet.

DOGS ARE FROM NEPTUNE

Operant vs. Classical Conditioning in Treating Aggression

My family (two adults and three children) has a seventeen-month-old Cocker/Border Collie mixed breed. We have had him since he was a puppy, and he was neutered at about five months. All seemed fine through his first spring and summer. We live in a rural area, and he saw few "outsiders" from age eight to thirteen months. At that point, I noticed aggressive behavior (lunging, snapping) at anyone he didn't know. He is never aggressive with family members; we are able to take food and toys from him. About two months ago I started using a "Snoot-Loop" to better control his head and mouth. This prevents him from reaching his target, but he won't relax just because I tell him to. He is less disturbed, and will allow people to get within 10 to 15 feet before he starts barking, and when he is at home in his crate, he will settle down within a few minutes as long as the stranger is not too close.

We recently finished a basic obedience class, where he was just great. Except for a little stiffness on the first night, he showed no aggression at all toward owners, dogs, or the trainer. He did, however, make a small lunge at an observing child who came to watch one class. We were not close enough for the child to even notice, but I could see and correct it (we were practicing the heel).

My thoughts are that: 1) the dog does not adjust quickly enough to changes in his surroundings, 2) the dog has not learned to enjoy the attention from others, and 3) he finds it his duty to protect me.

I do not want to restrain this dog for the rest of his life, but I also do not want anyone to get hurt. I would like to get him used to a muzzle and then get him closer to people without risking injury or fright. Eventually, I would like to have him loose in the house and yard, with a muzzle on when we have company. Do you think he can learn that people are fun to have around and that he does not have to drive them away? I have had dogs before, but this is a stumper. My eventual goal is to have him unmuzzled around our visitors.

10

AGGRESSION TOWARDS STRANGERS

Yes, I think it is possible to make significant gains in your dog's feelings about strangers. I also like your idea of doing some remedial socialization on-muzzle, with the eventual goal of having him off as well as your use of a Snoot-Loop to manage him on leash.

There are two ways to look at your dog's behavior and two ways to go about modifying it. The first is from a training or operant conditioning perspective. Behavior is under the control of its consequences. The behavior in this case is lunging and snapping. The reinforcer is some combination of the scary strangers keeping or increasing their distance from him (and maybe you), possibly the ability to act on a compulsion to herd moving stimuli and, possibly, inadvertent reinforcement from the handler. The solution offered by operant conditioning always involves becoming aware of and manipulating consequences.

For instance, a behavior mutually exclusive to lunging could be elicited in the usual context and reinforcement provided. Trainers often teach sit-stay or watch-me for food treats or tug toys to countercondition lunging. The number, scariness and proximity of the people is gradually increased, as the dog improves. Of course, food and praise are not the only reinforcers at work. The increase or maintenance of social distance is still potently reinforcing and can also be used to condition desired responses: lunging no longer works to make people go away, now sit-stay works. When trainers teach dogs to move away on their own when they feel uncomfortable about something, rather than behaving aggressively, it is an application of the same principle. The dog learns an alternative way of relieving the aversive of proximity to strangers: flight.

In your case, "sit & watch for treats" would be useful on the street. If you can recruit a couple of people who are strangers to the dog, you could do practice sessions to teach him the trick. Pass them at sufficient distance that you are able to get him to sit & focus on you by the fourth or fifth trial. Then gradually decrease the distance.

DOGS ARE FROM NEPTUNE

Another example of operant conditioning would be reinforcing the absence of lunging and snapping. This is different from counterconditioning in that there is no specific target behavior and, usually, no elicitation (prompting, targeting etc.): the dog is simply rewarded, regardless of what he is doing, provided he does not lunge. The common denominator, non-lunging, goes gradually up in probability.

A difficulty in shaping non-lunging is controlling the natural reinforcer of increased distance if the dog does engage in lunging. It is hard to find enough people with the necessary sang froid to stand their ground when a dog lunges at them. Therefore, it is important to control the intensity of the stimulus: keep those strangers far enough away that the dog can succeed at non-lunging a good deal of the time.

Another difficulty is execution. It is challenging for trainers, especially green trainers, to identify and reward *non*-behavior. It means rewarding sniffing the ground, scratching, trotting along rather imprecisely on leash etc. This can be painful for some trainers but they *must do it* if the dog makes the standard, i.e. fails to lunge in the stranger's presence.

Yet another example of operant conditioning is the crude but popular technique of punishing lunging and failing to punish non-lunging, with or without safety cues and positive reinforcement as adjuncts. This is most commonly seen as leash-correcting the dog for lunging and either ignoring him, praising him or food-treating him when he does not lunge. If the trainer's timing is good and the correction sufficiently aversive, lunging will often go down in probability. I label this crude because punishment is an invasive and side effect laden technique and is especially dangerous to use for problems relating to fear and aggression, as is the case here. Amazingly, many, many trainers seem oblivious to this down side to the technique.

There is a drawback to using operant conditioning as principle treatment in a case like this: it does not directly address the underlying emotion that motivates your dog, namely his discomfort

12

AGGRESSION TOWARDS STRANGERS

around strangers. Overt behavior may change but the conditions are still present for a resurgence of the problem later. You pruned the leaves but left the root. Plus, in the case of punishment, the underlying problem is usually worsened by the technique. The cost is a more intense and recalcitrant version of the problem up the road and/or a highly stressed dog. I have grave reservations about the use of punishment in cases like this on the sole basis of the effects of a no-win trap (lunge and you get punished, don't lunge and be too close to something which scares you - aversives either way) on a dog's health.

This leads us to the other perspective from which to approach your problem: classical conditioning. Fear and aggression are emotional responses. I often describe them as flip sides of the same coin. When your dog is near strangers, he is emotionally upset and will behave to turn off the sirens, red lights and warning buzzers going off in his brain saying "emergency!" This is what fight or flight is about. Whether the dog opts for fight (making the other guy move away with a lunge, snap, attack etc.) or flight (moving away himself) depends on his individual make-up and learning: what has worked in the past. If the first strategy doesn't work or is pre-empted, the dog will switch to the other.

Classical conditioning, which is basically learning by association, is very good at modifying emotional responses. All that is needed is for something you would like to condition (a Conditioned Stimulus or CS) to reliably predict something of intense relevance to the dog (an Unconditioned Stimulus or UCS), either positive or negative, depending on whether you want the dog to like or dislike what you are trying to condition. After a sufficient number of trials, the dog responds (and "feels") similarly to the CS as he does to the UCS. In your case, you need to pair strangers with whatever it is your dog likes the most in the world. This might be a certain kind of treat or a certain activity. Every time strangers are near, initiate this wonderful thing. You also need, to keep your association clear, to withhold this powerful goodie when strangers are not around.

13

DOGS ARE FROM NEPTUNE

It's best that the strangers be at a manageable level. If they are too close or intense, they may elicit aggression from your dog. So, ideally, you should work up a hierarchy from easiest to hardest case scenario. At home you might start with one passive stranger at twenty feet and work your way gradually up to a group of strangers noisily milling around all over the place near the dog, touching and feeding him (use a tube-shaped groomer's muzzle so that he can take treats). Be very reliable, providing the goodies to your dog regardless of how he behaves. Remember, you are not conditioning him to behave a certain way, you are convincing him that when strangers are around, his favorite thing in the world starts happening. I have found this technique works best when the goodies are provided even if the dog behaves badly, although I realize this feels like you are "rewarding" aggression at times.

This effort is well worth it. It is such a powerful technique that there is some speculation that part of the "punch" in operant techniques like counterconditioning and shaping the absence comes from the classical conditioning that takes place inadvertently: the association between the presence of the strangers and the high likelihood of rewards. The behavior the trainer tries to condition may actually be somewhat incidental, though it might buy time for classical conditioning to kick in.

So, why does your dog view a nearby unfamiliar person as an "emergency" anyway? The answer is always twofold: genetics and environment. Neophobia - fear of novelty - is an adaptive trait in animals. In domesticating dogs and other animals, one of the things we have selected for is ease of socialization - a greater willingness to accept environmental elements without spooking, essentially lower neophobia - but this is merely relative to a wild animal. They are still animals. And, if we slack off ever-so-slightly in applying selective pressure for an abnormal trait like extreme ease of socialization (which would make an animal less viable in a natural environment, resulting in reproductive disadvantage and thus be bred out in a few generations), neophobia pops back out.

AGGRESSION TOWARDS STRANGERS

With dogs, there is such hard pressure brought to bear on morphology that ease of socialization and other temperament traits are often skewed. Combine this with the inevitable genetic variability in a population, even with pressure to fix traits, and there will be individuals who are spookier, more "aloof," "reserved," lungy, shy, "loyal to their family," name your euphemism. It is hard to say how genetically predisposed your dog was to be wary of novel people as the smart money is on a strong environmental component in this particular case.

I agree with you that your dog's rural life has played a large role in his spookiness with strangers (refer to Suburban Dog Syndrome). A puppy with good genetics will often end up shy under suburban or rural day-to-day conditions, unless some effort is put in to get him around a good volume and variety of people on a regular basis. This is what I suggest you do with your dog. Lots of trips, regular visitors, classes (is there a sport he might enjoy like agility, flyball, free-style or obedience which takes place in a busy, class-type environment?) would all be extremely helpful, provided he has good experiences. The ideal intensity of environment would make him a bit tense at first with evident relaxation after a short while, very much like your obedience class experience.

So, the recipe I suggest for your dog is:

1) Precondition him to wearing a muzzle. Put it on for short periods, baby-talk him and tell him how cool and handsome he looks in it, give small food treats, then take it off and ignore him. Do this over and over until he seems happy to have the muzzle on. Gradually extend the time he wears it. Be careful with tube muzzles in hot weather - the dog can't pant, so don't leave it on indefinitely.

2) Use his favorite thing in the world - diced chicken breast, fetching his stuffed frog, you know what this is for your dog - and reliably provide it when strangers are around. It is best if you provide the goodie over and over while the strangers are present regardless of his behavior, provided he is relaxed enough to take the treat or play the game. When the strangers

go, end the activity. Do not provide it at other times. If the goodie is not muzzle-friendly, find one that is until you can work him off-muzzle.

3) You may also want to condition a behavior mutually exclusive to lunging and snapping, such as sit-stay/watch-me, using the special treats when it's in the presence of strangers. You could also teach him a trick to do when strangers first arrive at your house to give him a behavioral "security blanket." Eventually you could get the strangers to cue and reward the trick.

4) Avoid aversives. They produce exactly the opposite emotional response from what you are trying to achieve. Even if you succeed in suppressing lunging, the dog now has two reasons to dislike strangers: his original fear and now the fact that they reliably predict a higher likelihood of his being corrected. Classical conditioning works with aversives as well as goodies.

5) Passive, remedial socialization to strangers, i.e. exposure without necessarily providing goodies, is often helpful, provided it's at an intensity the dog can handle.

AGGRESSION TOWARDS STRANGERS

Growling Therapy Dog

My three-year-old Standard Poodle, Olivier, has started doing visits to a nursing home. The patients adore him. The problem is that he is unhappy around the employees in white uniforms. He even growled at one that approached him on our last visit. I was shocked and upset by this. Today he barked aggressively at a man in his tennis whites.

My dog's instructor told me that he is probably afraid of white uniforms and thinks that people wearing them are going to give him a shot. He associates them with being at the vet. She advised me to call my vet and arrange to take Olivier in for many visits: no shot, no blood work and no touching at first. I use the clicker, so when I get a good opportunity, I can click & treat.

I know that it wrecks any desensitization program to prematurely confront the dog with something he can't handle. I thought I had it all figured out. I was going to take my dog to the vet's for many visits. At first just stepping in the building. Then gradually working up to seeing the vet, then maybe getting patted by the vet.

When I called the vet to arrange the visits I also inquired about his next appointment for vaccines and heartworm: he is due and his visit is scheduled to take place in only two weeks.

How can I take him this soon for a shot and blood test, if I have not desensitized him to the vet and the white uniforms? Should I start the desensitization afterwards? When should I return to the nursing home? If we return soon I thought I should keep him away from the nurses station where he is most tense. I think he will be more relaxed in the activity room.

The patients really enjoy seeing him and I looked forward to our visits until his growling. I am concerned about going to the nursing home before I have done enough desensitizing, or going too soon after his next shot at the vets.

DOGS ARE FROM NEPTUNE

It's certainly plausible that Olivier is suspicious of white uniforms because they mean "vet" and "shots" to him. You don't mention whether he hates vaccinations or the vet (behaves fearfully there or growls at the uniformed staff), but I presume that this is the case.

There is also the possibility that he is spooked by the white-uniformed employees in the nursing home because it is an unusual picture for him. We should always remember that most dogs don't require negative experiences in order to be upset by something, they just need it to be sufficiently unusual.

I would venture that Olivier will not require formal desensitization to function well around the white uniforms, given the history. I would try some active remedial socialization first and, only if he doesn't improve or worsens, then go to a formal desensitization program. This would indeed require you to temporarily suspend visits to white uniform places that are too high up the hierarchy from the level he's at. You would commence after his annual shots.

I suggest you work directly. This means if your main goal is nursing home visits, your best course is to focus most of your energy on working him at the nursing home rather than at the vet's office. Now, if you do this, you will likely end up with a dog that is comfortable and happy at the nursing home but still tense at the vet's. In other words, you're setting up a discrimination: the white coats here mean shots, the white coats there mean fun, treats and socializing. If you would also like him to be more relaxed at the vet, you can work on the vet as a separate enterprise, exactly as you have contemplated.

Here's how to proceed with the nursing home:

1) There is no substitute for volume of exposure. Make regular visits, as often as you can. Make them extremely pleasant and have no official agenda other than getting Olivier used to the uniforms. For the first few visits, don't attempt any contact between the dog and the staff. Simply hang out in a moderate traffic area and pour on the praise and treats whenever the uniforms are around. Let him sniff around and explore if he

wants to. Maintain a relaxed, "good mood" demeanor yourself at all times. It is a good idea to avoid uniform-intensive areas like the nurses' station the first couple of times.

Observe him closely. How comfortable does he seem in general? How is he reacting to the uniformed passers-by? Is there anything else that spooks him: wheelchairs, gurneys, equipment, certain types of people, gaits etc.? Take detailed notes. Also, observe the trend. From visit to visit, is he more relaxed and comfortable? Or does he seem the same or worse?

2) In the meantime, rent a white uniform for a couple of days. These are available at costume stores. Wear it at home around Olivier. Behave normally. Make sure nothing terrible coincides with you wearing this uniform. For instance, if he is thunderstorm phobic, don't put it on on an afternoon when storms are predicted. Wear it continually until he shows zero anxiety about it. You can also do this with tennis whites or any other sort of unusual dress that spooks him.

3) After a few low-pressure visits to the nursing home, allow some proximity and contact with the employees. Hang out at the nurse's station. Again, watch for any signs of tension or fear. These can be as subtle as slight cringing, casual-looking avoidance, yawning, "lizard tongue" flicking, freezing and pupil dilation. Anyone who elicits this or more obvious signs like growling or active avoidance should be carefully noted. If any of the staff are willing, have them hand-feed him. People *love* giving cookies to dogs. If there is anything or anyone he doesn't like, go as often as you can and keep him at a "safe" distance (i.e. don't force contact), praising and treating him whenever the scary thing or person passes. If he seems to be "overheating" from accumulated exposure, use the activity room as a safe place to regroup before another foray.

The hardest thing about socialization is going at the dog's pace, however slow it may feel. Forcing him prematurely into contact with something that spooks him could make him worse.

DOGS ARE FROM NEPTUNE

4) If there turn out, from your observations, to be other triggers, tackle these individually. If wheelchairs are a problem, arrange for some extra exposure out of the nursing home context. Likewise, if a certain category of people makes him tense, seek it out for positive association (praise, treats) as often as possible. Many dogs are spooked by things like odd gaits as well as people holding, wearing or attached to unusual things (e.g. umbrellas, canes, ponchos, skateboards, pushing dollies, big hats etc.) and there is no shortage of these "pictures" in nursing homes. Dogs can also be spooked by people making sudden appearances from elevators or behind glass doors.

If there are *individuals* who are particularly scary, single them out for the very best treats. It is extremely important, as I mentioned, to go slowly, with no coercion whatsoever. If Olivier thinks these people are dangerous, pairing them with anxiety - which is what you get if you force him into greater proximity than he would voluntarily opt for - proves him right.

5) Incorporate some clicker training into the visits. This task-focus will have a relaxing and normalizing effect, provided your dog enjoys clicker training. Start with non-challenging behaviors and train in several areas of the building. Work up to training around his worst triggers.

Remedial socialization takes patience but is one of the most rewarding dog training endeavors. There is little that can match seeing one's previously unsure dog relaxed, confident and happy.

AGGRESSION TOWARDS STRANGERS

Suburban Dog Syndrome

Our English springer, Emma, three years old, has been with us since eight weeks. We got her while living in Istanbul and transported her back to the 12 at 12 months. She has been well behaved in our home, but reacts to visitors by barking and snapping. She is aggressive towards strangers when walking and even the neighbors whom she sees daily. We have attempted through the years to socialize her in public areas without results. She has been to obedience classes and responds to us when given commands, but never when a stranger or visitor is nearby.

At times she will growl at us when, for instance, she is sleeping and is disturbed. She even has bitten at night if kicked in bed. Emma also does not do well in kennels and has been labeled a "fear biter" by the vet.

Although we love Emma dearly (like a child), we are frustrated with the prospect of never having a dog that can be around people safely. This is our greatest concern. I have questioned our vet about her having some psychological problems and all she could recommend was a vet two hours away. What can we do?

You have two problems with Emma: aggression towards strangers and location-guarding/startle sensitivity. These may be completely independent or there may be a larger underlying mechanism at work. I will describe exercises you can do to address both problems, however I would also urge you to have Emma assessed by a vet-behaviorist or a certified behaviorist. Not only is it possible that a medication may make a dramatic difference, I really think you need someone with expertise to objectively and thoroughly check her out in person.

This will no doubt mean travel, perhaps even more than the two-hour trip to the vet you were referred to, but it will be well worth it. Follow-up can often be done by phone so it is unlikely that you will have to commit to a long drive more than once or twice.

DOGS ARE FROM NEPTUNE

The logical place to start a remedial socialization attempt is with the neighbors. It's not clear from your letter exactly what measures you have taken in this regard. Simply exposing the dog to strangers may not be enough for certain dogs or when a strong fear is in place, especially if the exposure is fleeting. Also, bear in mind that any coerced contact (e.g. having the dog on a leash while someone approaches or tries to pat her) would make her worse.

An important thing to understand is that many dogs that are undersocialized will not benefit much from occasional or fleeting exposure to novel situations. This is mainly useful for specific-case socialization. The assault with a generally spooky dog must be much heavier. The flaw in our thinking is that we use as yardsticks dogs who are relatively easy to socialize - a few walks as puppies to a park, a puppy socialization class, occasional guests to the home and poof, they're comfortable for life around strangers. When this style of socialization does not pay off, we pronounce some individual genetically unfit, non-plastic and give up. That style of socialization does not work for all dogs.

It's an interesting discussion that to breed for anything other than extreme ease of socialization is to breed genetically unfit pet animals. This is an important issue for breeders. They could decimate the number of spooky dogs in a few generations by breeding, without compromise, for extreme ease of socialization. Trainers, by contrast, come into the picture once dogs are already out there: we can't touch genetics in the cases we are presented. Environment is **our** tool to pick up the slack. It is my strong feeling that most, if not all, of these dogs have *some* plasticity (i.e. are temperamentally malleable) but that the amount of continuous pressure must be enormous. The evidence for this is correlation of fearful and aggressive animals, regardless of genetic type, with living situation and owner type.

The single variable that most affects a dog's day-to-day experience and exposure to novelty is where he lives. Think of the dog's genetic make-up as the constraints, or walls, around his potential. He can only grow so big, jump so high, live so long, and be so socialized. How close you get the dog to the wall depends on environment. And the weightiest ingredient on the "environment" cereal box is the dog's day to day grind.

Dogs who live in rural or suburban environments, see strangers occasionally if they are walked regularly and even less often in the form of delivery-people, guests etc. If the owner has a yard, this number goes down significantly. It's suburban dog syndrome again. An interesting exercise is to count the number of novel people (or other stimuli) a dog sees and calculate the per day average. Let's compare hypothetical two dogs, suburban dog Fluffy and downtown dweller Buffy.

If Fluffy gets thirty-minute walks up and down streets in the neighborhood seven times a week (a generous amount for any yard-owning suburbanite), she is likely to see completely new people sometimes. Let's be extremely generous and say she sees five new people per walk. The rest of her outings are to the fenced yard, where she sees the same neighbors when they are outside, if anybody. And let's say the family has six visitors that are new to Fluffy every two weeks (many weeks may go by with no one but familiar friends and family and then a huge party, so let's give it an average) and let's say delivery people or workmen come around and give cookies to Fluffy a couple of times a week (again, pretty generous). Fluffy goes to agility class once a week and sees another couple of dogs and people who are not familiar, on average, given the rapid turnover in the class. That's around fifty new people per week. Pretty good, right? Well, let's compare to an urban living dog.

Downtown dog Buffy has no yard and must go out onto the street to pee four times a day. There are 600 apartments in his high-rise, with an average of two people living in each apartment, for a total of 1200 people, not counting employees. There is a turnover of 5% per month, which means, 60 new people in the building, on average, each month. There are several similar buildings, an office complex, a hotel, a shopping complex, a police station, a university and a pedestrian street for restaurants and cafés as well as dozens of small businesses all within a few blocks of Buffy's building. Buffy sees, on average, twenty people per walk, most of them on the street, but several at much closer quarters in the elevator and lobby. That averages out to eighty new people per day or 560 per week. And that's just to go to the bathroom. If you factor in longer walks for exercise, visitors and any activities Buffy does, the figure goes way up. And the variety, as you might imagine, is pretty substantial. Get my drift?

The daily environment of these two dogs is profoundly different. No amount of punctuation, in the form of occasional outings, exercises, classes etc. could ever weigh up against this daily deluge. Punctuation style socialization - where the dog's main day to day experience is static but is punctuated by outings with novel stimuli - work when the dog's genetic potential is such that you can be miles from the "maximally socialized" wall and still have a livable animal. Where it doesn't work is with an animal whose genetic range is more at the spooky end of the spectrum. In such a dog, you need to be much closer to the "maximally socialized" wall to get a presentation you can live with. It's as though dogs like this spontaneously revert to their spooky state after each little blast of novelty if the socialization pressure is not constant enough.

Think of the dog's genetic potential for novelty-coping as a rubber band. Dogs who are easy to socialize have loose rubber bands. It doesn't take much pressure to stretch them. Dogs who are more difficult to socialize have tight rubber bands. It takes a lot of pressure to stretch them and, if the pressure comes off, they snap back. Constant-onslaught socialization keeps the pressure on the rubber band - day after day, year after year, no chance to snap back - until it gets stretched out and stays there.

Also, bear in mind that not very many suburban pets get anything close to what I've described for Fluffy. In semi-rural areas, dogs can go for days or weeks without seeing *any* new people. Amazingly, many people fail to see the significance. "Suddenly, out of the blue, without warning, unprovoked and for no reason, my dog bit an innocent guy on the street who merely held out his hand to be sniffed..." Suburban dog syndrome is at the root of many of these cases.

AGGRESSION TOWARDS STRANGERS

What I'm saying is that although you may feel like you've knocked yourself out socializing Emma, you're probably far from maxing out. And, if we would like dogs we suspect are genetically predisposed as spooks to be more sociable, we have no choice but to max out their socialization because the genetic envelope is already set. Obviously, it's impractical to change one's living situation ("hey! we'll move downtown!!!"), so we beef up socialization in other ways. The easiest is to use classical conditioning. This will give you the most bang for your buck, even if opportunities are limited (for more information on classical conditioning, see the previous questions in this section).

For your other problem, you will need to work on startle, aversive handling and placement commands. The MO is the same as for other sorts of resource guarding (covered in the next section): go up a hierarchy of difficulty in exercises for food treats, always building on success. But instead of object exchanges or food bowl, you will work on:

1) ordering her on and off sofas and beds (placement practice),

2) handling her in every conceivable way, even to the point of ouchiness (good enough treats and careful enough work will produce a dog who loves being pushed and pulled around) and

3) sneaking up on her when she's resting as well as waking her up when she's asleep in order to give her treats.

Work on these things separately before doing any combining. Make sure all adults in the house have done plenty of successful work before starting any supervised work with kids. If you have been giving lots of free treats, you will stop this devaluation of the resource and reserve it for exercises. And, most importantly, get yourself into the hands of a good behaviorist that can evaluate the whole picture in person and give you guidance.

DOGS ARE FROM NEPTUNE

RESOURCE GUARDING

Compulsive Food and Object Guarding

I have a little dog that guards objects. She no longer guards from me (because we've been working on it very hard), but from other dogs, other people and from no one (!). She will guard anything - the car, me, toys, the counter - when there is food on it. She even guards her food when she is the only one in the room (I can hear her doing this). She also stares at the walls, and digs & growls in her crate or the car. Again, when no one is around.

How far do I go with training before I know if I should discuss medication options with a vet? I don't like the idea, but she is a very sweet dog most of the time, and I am looking to place her (she & her brother came from a homeless woman). However, I am concerned that even if I work on and sort out the object guarding, she may not be safe with someone else. I don't want someone beating her if she does this with them or their dog. Any suggestions would be most helpful.

P.S. Her brother shows none of these behaviors, so I'm not sure it has to do with her having been on the streets.

As I read about your rescue dog, a few things sprang to mind that might be helpful. The wall-staring and the imaginary adversary guarding made some neuro/organic bells go off in my head. If your vet has behavior experience, I would certainly explore this route. If he doesn't, contact the American Veterinary Society of Animal Behaviorists. They can refer you to someone equipped to work up your case and, if indicated, prescribe and monitor medication.

Now, that said, there's nothing clinching the deal that this is necessarily an organic thing. Object guarding is often presented this pervasively - food AND toys AND owner AND locations, an all around paranoia - and could certainly develop to the point where it's done as a pre-emptive strike rather than in response to a dog's or person's approach. The mechanism for this is classical conditioning. If a certain context reliably predicts competitiveness over a resource, stimuli leading up to that context can get "infected" with the growly emotions.

A common example is mealtime in a multi-dog household where there are possessive types. It might begin with dogs guarding food from each other and then progress quickly to growliness while the meal is being prepared on the counter. The owner preparing the meal on the counter predicts mealtime, which is a Food-Guarding Occasion. The tension has gone back one generation. If the same dogs are always taken for a walk or let out before the meal preparation time, growliness might bleed back, for instance, to paw cleaning on the way in. Paw cleaning predicts meal-preparation, which predicts a Food-Guarding Occasion. And so on.

There are lots of cases of dogs fighting "for no reason" as some tension-laden event is led up to on a regular basis. A similar phenomenon which most dog owners are familiar with is car-whining. A few car trips to a place which is Too Exciting (dog park, lure coursing field etc.) often produces a dog who is whiny and carries on as you pull into the parking lot. A few more trips and the dog is antsy as the car approaches the place. A few more trips and the dog starts at the halfway point of the drive.

Back to your dog. It might be that in her life, food time has so reliably predicted a competitive event that guarding got hammered in to the point where another being is no longer necessary. The conditioned stimulus - food - is plenty to get the guarding behavior. The food guarding might have bled out to the other things - locations, toys etc. or they may have evolved quite independently, by similar means. The fact that her brother is not possessive is not a big head-scratcher even though he experienced a similar environment. The interplay between genetics and environment can produce some quite wildly divergent behavior in organisms. Subject eight human siblings to traumatic event X and watch as two become chronically depressed, one of which responds to

28

medication, the other marginally to psychotherapy; one develops a mild anxiety disorder but otherwise seems unaffected, two end up more successful than they probably would have been otherwise, two have psychosomatic problems and other assorted fallout and one appears completely unaffected until developing cancer twenty years later which we never know was related or not. Same experience, different outcomes. Level of complexity, very high.

In other words, your girl probably had a strong predisposition that achieved a rather full potential by the environment she was handed. She also may have a different degree of plasticity either overall or in this area than her brother. Rigid dogs are harder when it comes to disinstallation of behavior, no doubt about it. The other thing that bears mentioning is that we presume identical environments when this is not the case. Dogs in the same household (or, in this case, on the street), quite aside from their different genetic viewpoints, do not have identical experiences. They experience the rest of the pack without themselves in it and are not treated identically by their owners. Their own qualities bring out certain things in others and loops get formed and solidified. Individual relationships are complex, calling for different roles to be played and ruts to form. It's mind-bogglingly interesting.

I agree with you that she is a risky placement as is. And you're quite right that the progress you made with her will not necessarily generalize to anyone else. I would suggest two things:

1) try for more progress and greater generalization and

2) place her in a capable home (capable in the sense that they will continue exercises where you leave off or at least do maintenance, as well as not falling over in a faint if she growls or lunges at another dog. I would also suggest, with her history, a home with no kids).

I usually go all out treating possessiveness directed at people and manage or ignore it when it is directed at dogs. If she does not mangle dogs in the process of guarding against them, I would suggest you do likewise but, of course, it is a personal choice.

DOGS ARE FROM NEPTUNE

To get better generalization, you will want to get others to do the desensitization exercises that you have already made headway with. Also, cover all the bases: food dish, bones, randomly found food items, toys, car, yourself. I realize recruiting is tough but dog people are usually game. The people with more experience at training should practise with her first. The process goes more quickly with each successive person you add to her roster so the trainer-types can pave the way for the less experienced people.

Work with children only if she is muzzled, and only after you have covered several adults and she is clearly "getting" the game. You didn't mention if she bites and, if so, how severely. This is a big factor in determining how aggressively you can push the pace of treatment and whom you can recruit to work with her. If she's a strong biter, get her comfortable about wearing a muzzle before working the exercises with anybody.

I keep wondering how long you've had her. There is often a mitigating effect of simply being in a competent home, quite apart from any conscious efforts at training. Trainers who do in-home board & train know this. The dog won't produce the problem for the trainer though it does for the owner, the dog-sitter, the owner's friends etc. (in other words, it's more than a failure to generalize). Some combination of regular exercise, stimulation, structure & routine, containment and daily dog-human interplay fizzles the problem out before it gets presented even once in the trainer's home. This effect is also cumulative and therefore therapeutic for dogs with deeper problems, like yours. It may kick in slowly, however, and is usually not a full substitute for heavier artillery, like formal anti-guarding exercises.

If you make little or no headway in a few weeks, with other people doing regular exercises and you have had her in your possession for several months or more and the growling at her imaginary friend has not let up, I would then explore the medication possibilities. You may not have to go this route: it is significant that you were able to fix the guarding against yourself.

30

RESOURCE GUARDING

Object Guarding and Children

My dog recently bit my three-year-old daughter when she took a bone from him. He did not bite hard, but enough to scare her and me. I already know now not to leave him with others unsupervised.

My question is twofold:

1) What path do I take in socializing him to children? I do not want to put my daughter at risk trying to verify whether he is cured.

2) What reliability can I expect? I do not want to put my daughter at risk.

Notice the common theme. Also, I am now working him daily and will do whatever it takes to get him to as close to 100% reliable as I can.

I hear you.

I am not sure whether socialization to children is the problem here so much as resource guarding. Resource guarding is often person-specific, which would explain why your daughter seems singled out. It is also possible that your dog would guard things from a broader spectrum of people but that your daughter is the only one who has stumbled onto this so far. Kids are often the first to discover the family dog is possessive.

Here is how to proceed: start working on object guarding, with you paving the way for your daughter. When you (and all other adults in the household) have completed the exercises successfully, your daughter may begin the same sequence under your supervision. Before she starts, take the time to get your dog comfortable wearing a groomer's muzzle (in fact, make him actively like it by selectively providing special treats when he has it on - don't start the OG exercises with your daughter until he is relaxed and happy with the muzzle on).

She can then complete her progression of exercises with the dog on-muzzle. When she has gone all the way through successfully, repeat from the beginning off-muzzle. This means, by the time she is working the dog off-muzzle, the reliability will be very good. Do it this way even if the dog has only ever guarded against your daughter.

The basic exercise is called an object exchange:

1.   take an object away from the dog

2.   give him a really, really good treat you had hidden in your pocket or pouch (never bribe by showing it to him up front)

3.   give the object back to the dog

4.   repeat several times in a row

5.   also do spot checks at random times – give the surprise treat but do only one repetition

Practise a few sessions with boring objects the dog has never guarded to establish the pattern. Give it to him, take it away, supply the fringe benefit, give the thing back. Over and over. We want him doing exchanges in his sleep. Then, do your best to rank, in order of how "hot" they are (i.e. how likely the dog is behave possessively around them), objects your dog guards. The list should include his toys, bones, anything he has ever guarded as well as forbidden and novel items like laundry, garbage etc.

Starting with the easiest first, practise exchanges on each item until the dog is perfect. Spot-check it to make sure he is perfect on the first repetition any time, any place. Then start working on a new object, one higher on the list. When you have completed every object, change handlers and start at the easy, random objects again. The second person will usually progress more quickly up the hierarchy. If the object guarding is person-specific, that person(s) should go last. Their progress may be more gradual so be patient. The spot checks will really come into play when you have reached the level of working on bones etc. and the dog is spontaneously chewing one. This is harder than an exchange in the context of a series of exercise reps where the dog is "warmed up."

In severe, compulsive guarders, we ration their food so that, if they want to eat, they must voluntarily give up objects. These increases in motivation is helpful if progress is slow in general, slow for a particular object or slow for a certain individual. Don't be afraid to let the dog go hungry for a day if he won't do nice exchanges. Don't get mad, just say "too bad for you," walk away and try again tomorrow. If you are getting frequent guarding, it means you are trying to go too fast. Relax the pace: repeat previously successful levels and insert intermediate steps between your last success and your problem level. Good tinkering is what separates mediocre from great training here.

Once his confidence about relinquishing objects grows, the dog's rations can be returned to normal. The goal is for a formerly paranoid dog to absolutely love and look forward to you taking things away from him. It is a fabulous transformation to behold. When he is perfect, you may cease practice sessions and simply spot check regularly. Maintenance is important: if you slack off on the spot checks, expect regression.

I would also suggest you do exercises for food-bowl, handling and location guarding as these often occur in constellation with object guarding. If any are not "hot" for your dog, you will simply race through the progression. Better safe than sorry, so let's rule everything out.

Children are not necessarily an independent risk factor here. He may be well socialized to children and still an object guarder. To assess whether he's thoroughly socialized to kids, look for clues in his history. The questions to ask are:

DOGS ARE FROM NEPTUNE

- Would you say your dog likes your daughter? (is your "yes" enthusiastic or non-committal)

- Would you say your dog likes children?

- Has the dog ever been aggressive (growl, snarl, lunge, snap) towards your daughter in any context other than when he was in possession of a resource?

- Has the dog ever shown signs of being uncomfortable around or fearful of your daughter or of children in general?

- Was the dog around children from the time of his birth until around 4 months of age? If so, were his experiences good ones? How many kids? Would you have described him as "outgoing" with children? ("aggressive, intolerant, assertive, fearful, aloof, ignores" are all bad answers here)

- Does the dog greet your daughter excitedly, wagging, wiggling and licking or is he standoffish with her after an absence? How does his greeting for her compare with his greeting for you?

If there are issues about children aside from the object guarding, you will have some extra work to do here. The prognosis for remedial socialization to children depends somewhat on your dog's individual make-up and his age, younger dogs being, as a rule, more plastic. If he is seriously undersocialized to children, address this before commencing the resource-guarding exercises with them. To minimize risk, again, take the time to get the dog happy wearing a muzzle for anything involving close contact. It may take many months of relentless association of children with the biggest reinforcers in his life to get deep change but this is absolutely necessary.

If it is strictly object guarding (and its other partners in crime, food-guarding, location-guarding and handleability), the expected outcome is less dependent on your dog's age. Object guarding can usually be brought under control and kept at bay with reasonable confidence in dogs of all ages, provided you are diligent about the exercises.

The other factors that affect prognosis are owner compliance and the severity of the dog's mouth. Terrific compliance in aggression cases is both necessary and hard to come by. Changing underlying emotional responses takes much longer than adding behaviors to the repertoire, as is the case in other kinds of training. It is hard for owners to stick with a demanding program that does not bear fast fruit. Luckily, it sounds like you are motivated and committed. A soft mouth, such as seems to be the case with your dog, is always a huge boon to the cause. It allows for a more aggressive treatment pace, less chronic worry about the implications of re-offense and usually means a less damaged bond between owner and dog, especially if the bite was intra-familial.

Soft mouth is best installed in puppies by supplying abrupt time-outs for hard bites. If dogs arrive at adulthood with hard mouths, it is possible, using selective reward, to teach them to do things like take treats gently from your hand but it usually requires a "reminder" cue ("gently" etc.). Their "default" setting, especially under duress, often remains barracuda mode. This is why it is so critically important to install bite-inhibition in puppies.

It's important to understand that there is only one way to guarantee your dog, or any dog, will never bite: put them to sleep. **All dogs**, including those without histories of biting, are at risk, just as all people are at risk to, for instance, lose it and be rude to someone in the bank or in traffic. Imagine a day where you lose your job, have a toothache or get served with divorce papers. On top of it you didn't get enough sleep the night before. You have a phobia of insects and there is a spider in the car with you on the way home.

If someone cut you off on the road that day, resulting in a collision, you would probably be very upset and behave badly. Hopefully you wouldn't physically assault the other driver. This would be crossing the line in most peoples' opinion. But everyone would empathize with some pretty harsh words. When dogs growl, snarl, snap and bite without damage, this is, in dog society at least, not over the line. The line is crossed when a dog inflicts an injurious bite. Another human analogy is the difference between suing someone and hitting them. Both aggressive acts. One legal, one not.

It is also noteworthy that most "well-bred" people, at some point in their lives, come under sufficient stress to make them lose their temper, be rude, say hurtful things to a loved one and regret it later, contact a lawyer, write a heated letter of complaint etc. It is the rare person, however, who takes a firearm and deals with their anger with serious violence. Likewise, there is a major distinction between damaging and non-damaging aggression in dogs. The tricky thing is that our goal is to have *zero* dog to human aggression, even of the most ritualized sort. To meet this high standard requires many lines of defense.

The first line of defense is genetics: breed for ease of socialization, low resource guarding, high handleability, low reactivity and low assertiveness. Most breeding stock is not actively screened for most of these, unfortunately. Morphology is usually the paramount breeding criterion. The next lines of defense involve early intervention. Get the puppy around a wide, wide variety of people and dogs from day one. Do plenty of handling and gentling. Systematically soften up the dog's mouth. Do object exchanges, food bowl exercises and lots of hand feeding. Attend puppy classes, institute "nothing for free" policies and maintain socialization. All this is much lower on the hit list of most puppy owners than things like housetraining, chewtraining and basic manners so is often neglected.

Another line of defense is to carefully protect the dog you have built: maintenance of socialization, maintenance of soft mouth, resource spot-checks and handling. Avoidance of trauma and abuse. Good overall physical and mental health maintenance. Swift touch-ups at the first sign of any slippage. Keeping our heads out of the sand by remembering that all dogs are at risk. All dogs.

Yet another is public education. There needs to be massive improvement in people's knowledge about how to behave around strange dogs. They are, unfortunately, still guided by myths.

Like in the human analogy, there is often a combination of elements that conspires to produce the aggression on some occasion. In your dog's case, you definitely know about object guarding. You are also going to rigorously screen for other forms of resource guarding and handleability (being grabbed, hugged, nudged, shoved, restrained, groomed, startled, and touched on all areas of the body) as well as ruling children in or out. Other things to screen for are strangers - especially strange children, approach and hands (for instance, head ducking).

There is nothing more rattling than bites to children. They are at greatly increased risk because they are often not adequately covered as a specific socialization base. Kids also often push their luck with dogs more than adults do and are more vulnerable because of their size: they take it to the face more often than we adults as well as being more fragile. What a recipe. I sure understand your concern.

Some parents find that no amount of competence and prudence is sufficient given the no-guarantee clause and therefore elect to not own dogs. Others are extremely cavalier. Most fall somewhere in the middle, installing as many lines of defense as they can but still opting to have a dog. It is difficult to say with authority whether your dog is an unqualified prospect (age, breed, history gaps), but his mouth sounds good and, if his overall relationship with your daughter is also good, I would say your chances are excellent.

DOGS ARE FROM NEPTUNE

Food Guarding

I have an eighteen month old PWD who started showing food aggression towards our other dogs when he was about ten months old. We did go to puppy kindergarten and then handling classes followed by some shows until late fall. I separated him from the rest of our dogs because he would attack them if he thought there was something on the floor that the other dog was sniffing or chewing at. There were never serious injuries but, because I show, I didn't want them to have teeth marks on their faces. He was allowed to play outside with two other female dogs. Since then he has been allowed to eat his supper upstairs with us. Now he has become territorial when my husband moves around the kitchen, especially near his dish. He has lunged at him, snapping and growling.

My husband is afraid of him after this latest development. I have had him feed the dog from his hands and he is fine with that. The dog is actually quite gentle when he takes food from anyone. The other night the dog was licking dishes in the dishwasher when my husband approached. The dog lunged at him, growling and snapping until I pulled him off. I then took him downstairs to the kennel. This is the first time that I have had a food aggression problem.

We kept three dogs from this litter. The other boy is not food aggressive at all, nor is the female who lives with another family.

There is universal agreement among trainers and behavior people that aggression directed at people should be addressed (although there is some diversity of opinion regarding how to proceed). There is less agreement on the dog to dog aggression problem - whether to intervene (and, again, more diversity of views regarding how) or simply stay out of it. My policy with dog to dog resource guarding is to intervene with behavior modification and management when there are injurious fights and/or a greatly elevated incidence.

RESOURCE GUARDING

Your boy sounds like an enthusiastic food guarder. He has done some pre-emptive strikes or "mugging:" attacks or displays at another dog who is in possession of a resource as opposed to guarding only when he himself already had control of the resource. This is the bad news. The good news is he lives in dog-land and has a play history. He is therefore at low risk for inflicting a damaging bite (although I empathize with your concern about face marks on your other dogs - even an inhibited bite will often leave a mark on a head or muzzle). Depending on the frequency of altercations between him and the other dogs over other resources, I would probably opt for some management of the social groups, as you have been doing, especially around "hot" times like mealtimes.

The bigger issue is your husband. You didn't mention whether you yourself had any difficulty around the dog's food dish; I would guess you have much less. The way I suggest you approach the problem is for both you and your husband to do exercises with the dog. You will pave the way for him by doing each level of exercise first so that the dog gets some rehearsal before your husband starts. It will probably still be trickier for him. The severity of resource guarding is often person-specific.

The hand feeding he has already been doing is excellent. The next step is to rehearse an extremely low-intensity version of the problem scenario: dog, food and hubby all in close proximity. Then, the resemblance to the real problem situation will be gradually increased. The intensity can be lowered in a few ways:

1) greater distance between both hubby and dog as well as between dog and food

2) low attractiveness of the food item you are using

3) low resemblance to normal context (i.e. new food dish, different room, and different time of day)

So, if the worst case scenario is the dog in possession of a highly coveted food item at his regular mealtime in the kitchen (so he has had some "wind-up") and your husband approaching directly with his hand out, an ultra-easy first approximation might look like this:

You are in the living room at a time of day removed from mealtime. There are no other dogs around. The dog is on a sit-stay ten feet from a piece of cardboard (pre-examined by the dog) and you have your hand already on the cardboard.

Now you can do the exercise. It goes like this:

1) say "thank you"

2) pick up the piece of cardboard

3) praise the dog and give him a treat (from your pocket or pouch, never shown up front)

4) put the cardboard back down where it was, keeping your hand on it

5) repeat ten times in a row

Then have your husband, under your supervision, do his set of 10 reps.

If there is no hint of tension from the dog and he is clearly enjoying getting the treats, progress to the next exercise. This rule - move up in difficulty only when you have absolute perfection at the level you're already on - is a cornerstone of desensitization. If you get a regression, back up and review the previous level to get back on track.

Here is a possible progression of exercises for a food guarder:

• Same exercise, but with an approach component. Abandon the cardboard and approach it before doing the sequence above ("thank you" etc.)

• Do it five feet away from the dog

- Do it with the cardboard right in front of the dog (if necessary, omit the approach component initially and leave your hand on the cardboard, then add the approach)

- Do it in the kitchen

- Do it in the kitchen right after the dog's dinner

- Do it in the kitchen right before the dog's dinner

- Go back to the working in the living room. Change the cardboard for an empty dog supper dish (a different one than he is used to) and do exercises 1 - 7

- Go back to the living room again and do exercises 1 - 7 with a food item in the new supper dish. The food item should be considerably less preferred than the treats you are using to reward his tolerance. The goal is to touch the dish and then give the reward. Don't worry if he eats what's in the dish

- Do 1 - 7 with a slightly nicer food item

- Practise, from a distance flipping special bonuses into the dog's supper dish while he is eating a normal meal

- Gradually decrease the distance you flip from until you are dropping the bonuses in the dish, hanging around while he eats, removing the dish to add really good bonuses.

There are many variations on these exercises, "dishwasher" being one for you. This is but one suggested sequence. The goal is to end up with a dog that not only tolerates but also loves and anticipates approaches when he is eating.

If there is a sticky point, try to insert intermediate levels of difficulty between your last successful version and the one you're stuck on. The greater the volume of trials you do per session, the better (you may do more than 10 if you have time). This behavior has a huge genetic component so you are "swimming upstream." Don't forget to pave the way for your husband by warming up the exercise with your reps first. When the dog gets slick at it, you may let your husband go solo but do play it conservatively at first. Unraveling this sort of resource paranoia takes some patience.

I can't overemphasize the benefit of going very **slowly** and **gradually** in the early sessions. Take a patience pill and get some guaranteed successes under your belts. Interestingly, if you play your cards right in the early sessions, you will fly through the more difficult exercises later on, whereas if you push the pace early on, you may never really win the dog over and you crash and burn on the harder stuff. What usually confounds attempts to desensitize dogs around resources is an arbitrarily set pace. Another error is not having better goods on you than you are exchanging for (this seems like a no-brainer but you'd be amazed at the number of people who mangle this part).

If at any point you get aggressive behavior, abruptly end the session, give the dog the cold shoulder and re-commence later at your last successful level. Some trainers beef up motivation by making the dog earn most or all of his caloric intake in exchange exercises (thus increasing the potency of the consequence if the dog screws up - he goes hungry for a day). My suggestion is to try cutting his normal ration down 20 or 25% and making him earn this portion during exercises before considering the more drastic 100% "work to eat" regime.

Once the behavior is at bay, maintain it with regular spot checks: approaches to his dish with bonuses, hanging around the dish and adding bonuses, removing the dish to add extra special bonuses. Bear in mind that the tolerant behavior may not necessarily generalize to other people aside from you and your husband. If you want to add people to the roster (and even eventually get a more global attitude adjustment from him) have novel people do reviews - this may go quickly (a couple of reps per level) and, for certain people, it may bog down, necessitating a slower pace. Supervise new people closely.

Handleability

I have a dog that is seven months old. He is loving and obedient except when I try to brush or comb him. He will get a cold, "glassy," far-off look in his eyes as I start and then tries to bite my hand if I continue. Once he snapped at me when I picked him up suddenly. Although none of these attacks has broken the skin, I am worried he eventually will.

We began training him at six months and were told he thinks he is dominant over me. Therefore, when he does this, we were to take hold of the sides of his face, lift his front end off the ground and stare into his eyes, in order to make him submit. We did this several times and he became worse. Now he urinates if I reach towards his head area and has started growling as soon as he sees the brush. The last time I tried to reprimand him, he bit my face. The trainer said to hold him down on his back or have a leash and choker on him all the time but I fear I am ruining my relationship with this dog. Someone suggested I would have been better off starting this training at an earlier age. Would it have made any real difference if my dog is dominant? Where do I go from here?

Trainers differ as to how readily they invoke the concept of dominance to explain behavior and develop training strategies. My main problem with dominance is that is a presumption of motive rather than a description of events. In your case, the problem is the dog cannot be easily handled or groomed. An attempted explanation of this observation such as the dog defending his rank status by disallowing more junior members of the pack to perform certain operations – e.g. grooming – on him, while logically defensible is, I suspect, empirically wrong.

A substantial portion of dogs that bite their owners are diagnosed with dominance aggression. Sometimes this diagnosis leads to interventions such as work-to-eat regimes, handling desensitization and object exchanges which fix the problem and sometimes to risky "hold him down"/"shake him by the scruff" type techniques which have a worse track record.

DOGS ARE FROM NEPTUNE

Both these approaches to treatment are better explained in terms of learning theory. Shaking and holding them down are aversives for most dogs. If aversives are sufficiently strong, they reduce the probability of the behavior that precedes them. So, if something like an alpha roll technique worked, did it work because the dog felt "dominated" or because behavior preceding a strong enough aversive goes down in frequency? Parsimony laws dictate in a case like this that we rule out learning laws before entertaining arguments based on complex social structure concepts like dominance.

Progressive desensitization – exchange hierarchies, handling exercises, placement practice – works extremely well to reduce or eliminate behaviors like object guarding, poor handleability and location guarding. Again the question is: does it do so because it operates on the dog's perception of his rank in the pack or because of a well-executed exploitation of learning principles? And, again, I would want to rule out the obvious first: dogs that are unhappy about being handled, startled and having things taken away from them can be improved with desensitization to the situation that makes them uncomfortable.

I wonder if dominance is sometimes confused with leverage. Both aversives and reinforcers such as food, play and attention supply trainers with leverage over dogs. You can't control someone's behavior unless you control things of importance to them. This goes for negotiations, fascist dictatorships and controlling our loved ones, in this case dogs. You must give and remove good things and/or inflict and remove bad things.

In the case of reinforcers, deprivation increases motivation. When owners hand out food, play and other reinforcers for free, the dog is less inclined to work for them. This bogs down not only obedience training but exercises like object exchanges, placement and handling.

So, in order to get maximum progress, key reinforcers can be rationed or withheld. Some trainers and behavior people view this as kind of a more sophisticated version of "putting the dog in his place," adjusting attitude this time not with alpha rolls and collar corrections, but with reinforcer rationing. It seems needlessly obfuscating to do this however. Why not simply say we are bumping up motivation in order to expedite work on the problem?

Okay, on to your dog. You need to work on making him enjoy being handled. The key is to start off with something he is fairly comfortable with already and progress gradually to more difficult kinds of handling. A good way to get organized is to the separate elements of:

- Body part: where on his body are you working? Is it somewhere he does not mind being touched or his worst area?

- Invasiveness: what kind of procedure are you doing? Are you just gently massaging or are you restraining him and pulling mats out?

- Tools: are you using equipment he already has a problem with such as nail clippers, brush or comb?

Create a hierarchy, from easiest to most difficult, in each of these areas. Remember that the "easiest" level must be something he is *already good at*. For dogs that will not allow their nails to be clipped, it might mean starting out on the shoulder, with gentle massaging. The nail clippers are twenty feet away on a table in this first session.

Beginning work with so distant an approximation of the final product is tough for some handlers. But it is essential. Although the handler has a mental image of what real nail clipping should look like, it does no good to start with a closer approximation of this final rung of the hierarchy if the dog behaves fearfully or aggressively.

The basic procedure is to first do a little of the exercise and then, if successful, give the dog a reward. If the dog is highly motivated by fetch or tug, you can do a fetch or tug break. If the dog is highly

DOGS ARE FROM NEPTUNE

food motivated, you can use food. If your dog is neither a big eater nor a compulsive toy maniac, I suggest you beef up his motivation by suspending or reducing his meal ration. How much should you ration? The answer is based on motivation and the desired result: how cool is the dog about your offering and how badly do you want to fix the problem? You must also use extremely palatable treats. This "heavy artillery" treat should never be offered at any other time and should be sufficiently nutritious that it can serve to temporarily make up the deficit created by the meal rationing. It is shrewd to have several kinds: diced turkey breast, freeze dried liver, cheese tortellini, garlic croutons etc. etc.

Let's say your dog will tolerate being stroked on his head, shoulders and back when he is on your lap but will not tolerate being touched anywhere else on his body, nor allow touches to his head, shoulders or back under any other circumstances. He also will not tolerate grooming equipment closer than six feet away.

To work on body parts, begin with him on your lap. Stroke him several times where he tolerates it, then praise him and give him a treat. Repeat a couple more times, then extend your stroke very slightly onto a leg. When he tolerates it, praise him, give him a treat and do it again. If he growls or snaps, you went too far too fast. End the session, cool off, regroup and try again later.

Every time he tolerates something well, move to a trickier part of his body, always being very gentle. Always follow up with the treat. Do not offer the treat up front as a diversion or bribe. He wins it if he fulfills his part of the bargain: tolerating the handling. If you do enough of this, he will actually look forward to the sessions. Your demeanor is important; the best way to approach it is as a game you are offering to play with the dog: "If you're lucky, we'll play the body touch for prizes game..."

You will also need to work on touching him in other contexts, always for the special treats. After you have made some headway on your lap, start seeing how close you can get your hand to him at other times. Look closely for signs of freezing up ("glassy" eyes etc.) as this is, in your dog, the first sign that he is tense. If you see any, back off and try something easier for a few trials before pushing the envelope again. Dogs who issue warning signs like freeze-ups, growling and snarling are better to work with than dogs that do not because you know with the former when you are getting onto thin ice.

When you have covered all body parts, re-start the easy body parts, but this time experiment with different kinds of handling: gentle grabs, restraint, pulling, pushing, poking etc. Always start off with a guaranteed success and then carefully increase difficulty. As he gets to know the game, you will find you can escalate more quickly but in the early days, go *gradually*. Remember, too, that he is coming off some quite scary attacks from you recently (the face grabs) so it may take a little longer to build his confidence back up about humans grabbing him. He will think it means bad news.

To work on the grooming gear, a good way to start off is to just have it lying around on the floor. Every time he goes near it or, better yet, investigates it, praise (a clicker would be valuable here) and give him a treat. As a next step, hold a grooming tool in your hand but do not try touching him. Simply sit with the brush/comb/nail clippers and a pile of treats. Every time he comes near, praise and flip him a treat. When he is at the point where he is right next to you and you are hand-feeding him treats as fast as he will take them, start moving the brush around. If he spooks or growls, just ignore it, wave it around a few more times and then wait quietly for him to pull himself together and approach again. When he does, repeat the movement. Do this procedure until he stands and eats while you wave grooming equipment around.

Then try touching him with it. Not grooming him, just touching him once with the piece of equipment. Make it a game: "I touch you with Mr. Scary Metal Comb and You Win a Prize!" Patience is the most valuable quality you can have for this endeavor. Luckily, it's a fun and interesting process that will zip along nicely once you start gaining his trust. Some people have a natural knack for progressive desensitization and others find it taxes their patience.

DOGS ARE FROM NEPTUNE

The odds are that you would have had much easier time gentling your dog to routine handling and grooming if you had started when he was young. Socialization, anti-resource guarding exercises and handling all benefit immensely from early training. Unfortunately, the word is not fully out yet about puppy classes and many people do not begin working seriously on their dog until he is six months old or more. In the case of socialization, it is, of course, catastrophic to postpone it this long.

I would like to see competently run puppy classes, which are usually restricted to puppies that have had at least two rounds of shots, extended to younger puppies. Admittedly, there a definite risk associated with incompletely vaccinated puppies being out of quarantine, and veterinarians and trainers must continue to inform owners of this.

There is also a risk associated with postponing socialization and training. Most owners are unaware of this risk. I feel it would be more responsible to fully disclose **all** risks and potential benefits to puppy owners so that they can make fully informed decisions about whether they wish to quarantine their puppies or take them to courses designed for six to ten week olds.

It is possible that the number of dogs lost to disease in such classes would be outweighed by the number saved from eventual euthanasia due to behavior problems. Of course, the condition of entry into these kinds of puppy classes would be full disclosure of potential risk. No one would be obligated to go. They would just be informed of their choices.

In your case, the early start issue is water under the bridge. There is no point agonizing about it. Your chances of a good resolution are excellent. Be sure to also check for resource guarding (toys, bones, food-dish, sofa) as these often appear hand in hand with handleability problems.

DOG – DOG AGGRESSION

Defending Space

My dog was attacked twice before he was a year and a half (once at six months, once at just over a year). He is now almost two and a half, and has defensive aggression. At the off-leash dog park, he is afraid of large dogs and while greeting them, will sometimes bark and snap at them. I'm assuming this is to back them off (the best defense is a good offense?). It usually works, so he is reinforced for doing it.

I have tried positive reinforcement when he greets a dog nicely, and I have tried punishment when he barks (bopping him under the chin). The punishment results in him not coming to me after he has done this, so punishment isn't working!

I feel I have to teach him what is appropriate behavior, but I also have to teach him what is inappropriate. I don't want him to do this to the wrong dog someday and have him get into a fight. Do you have any suggestions on how to curb this fear aggression?

He is a Pharaoh Hound, neutered at six months. He loves to play, but is very cautious around big dogs (even though he is just as big as they are!).

I would guess your interpretation is correct, i.e. that he is uncomfortable with the proximity of large dogs and behaves the way he does to protect his immediate space. You can probably improve his confidence by experimenting with the following.

He needs some easier experiences thrown at him to start weakening the association between large dogs and the chemical brain bath he has been having in their presence. You can do this by manipulating the distance of dogs likely to scare him, the size of the dogs he meets, the number of dogs he encounters at once or in rapid succession and the behavior of the dog towards him. The idea is that if dogs are presented to him at a lower intensity, the barking and snapping won't be triggered and he will start to experience and expect to experience non-frightening emotions when big dogs are around. You will have broken the vicious circle (dog approaches - snap - dog backs off - whew! see, it works). Then you can gradually bump up the level of difficulty, contingent on continued relaxed behavior.

The problem is implementing this in a dog park. You have no control. So there's a trade-off there: some good experiences that keep his social skills polished and keep a positive association alive with certain dogs, and some experiences which may be perpetuating the cycle. Try increasing his percentage of successes with big dogs in a situation where you have greater control.

For instance, if you had access to a friend's large dog, you could arrange trials of gradually decreasing distance, by leashing the other dog (don't use an on-leash lunger type). The most useful variation would be to do sessions with dogs you already know he has a problem with. Or, if you knew anyone with a huge, friendly, passive dog, you could invite them over for extended off-leash desensitization sessions in a yard where there are no other dogs to complicate things. Then, work your way up a hierarchy of dogs as his confidence increases. Then try two dogs at a time in the yard. Then try the dog park at a slow time of day etc.

Combat the negative emotion by substituting, over and over again, another feeling: this is the "open bar" technique. Continue to frequent the dog park. Teach him that big dogs are a wondrous thing to have come up to him, because they cause the bar to open: you start baby-talking him and produce a special, coveted food reward that he never gets under any other circumstance.

This is not "shaping the absence" (selectively rewarding nice interactions) because the bar opens regardless of his behavior towards the other dog. This is sometimes a hard technique to agree to do because it feels like you are rewarding anti-social behavior at times. The best way to think about it is to imagine the classical conditioning effect (large dog = open bar) as overriding operant conditioning (this behavior = this consequence). For underlying emotion ("I am not comfortable with big dogs") to change, the association (large dog = open bar) must be made strong. The strength of association is maximized when:

- the bar opens *every time* large dogs are around
- the bar closes right after they leave
- the bar consists of something very special the dog does not get in any other circumstance
- nothing else makes the bar open

The closer you can hit 100%, the better. This is how the dog will notice the trend. Keep it up - it could take weeks or months to get a significant dent. You can combine both 1 and 2, especially if you are unable to make yourself baby talk and food-reward a dog that is barky or snappy. Easier dogs and/or dogs controlled at a distance will allow you to open the bar without any accompanying growliness.

Another way around your own possible reluctance to open the bar regardless of behavior is to laugh or giggle at the dog (Campbell's "jolly routine") when he is tense and snappy, rather than succumbing to the urge to punish. Punishing gives him extra reasons to dislike dogs aside from his original one(s): large dogs get him in trouble and make his owner tense (again, note that *association is everything* here). I've often observed owners when their dogs meet other dogs and wondered whether their well-meant admonitions ("be NICE...eeeeeasy...be GENTLE...") come across to their dog, who is wholly focused on the coming interaction, as, at best, a general sense of tension back there on the other end of the leash or, at worst, threats directed at the approaching stranger.

Giggling is not only tone-setting but the "laugh at your dog" instruction gives the owner an alternative behavior to threats and reprimands, which we know are counterproductive (basically, give them anything to do but threaten and reprimand - as an aside, it would be interesting to study aggression incidence as a function of owner instructions such as "do a cartwheel" or "sing Hail to the Chief" and compare this to the jolly routine, punishment and doing nothing/ignoring the behavior). It is also the standby when bringing out food rewards at the dog park elicits competitiveness among the dogs there.

There are inevitably two problems in cases like this: the dog's behavior and the resulting public relations fiasco. Sometimes I think part of what drives the endless punishing of dog-dog aggression is owner embarrassment: a desire to do the right thing vis à vis the other dog owners present and a need to do something with the negative emotion of "how dare you embarrass me". We empathize with other owners: the horror of having one's dog snapped at and then watching the owner of the aggressor be happy and bubbly. "What will the other owners think?" "You shouldn't let him get away with that!" This kind of social pressure is significant and must be taken into consideration as it really handcuffs dog owners from effective intervention. I am appalled at how owners of dogs with quite minor dog-dog problems are ostracized by other owners. The best way to eventually overcome it is to keep bringing it out into the open.

DOG - DOG AGGRESSION

Lunging and Chronic Fighting

Mufasa is a fourteen month-old male, neutered boxer (65 lbs. and VERY athletic) that we acquired as a seven week old puppy. We put a high emphasis on socialization, and he is flawless (except for jumping up and over-exuberance) around people of all ages, sizes, shapes, colors, etc. He displays no "possessiveness" over his toys, food, or "space" and has had about one hour of off leash supervised play every day since he was over his shots. Although we (adults ONLY) frequently wrestle and "play fight" with him, we have had extremely good results in inhibiting his bite reflex (he has never broken skin on a primate or canine) and he displays an extremely "soft mouth". We take every opportunity to burn off his ample energy, and he is a well-balanced part member of his extended primate family. Overall, he has been exposed to HUNDREDS of dogs (mainly in an off leash dog-park setting), he attended puppy classes and he has now begun obedience training. Perfect, right?

Our only (and significant) concern is that his rambunctious manner (or lack of manners) has consistently earned him growls, snarls and the occasional nip from older dogs, and that he is now NOT backing down from these well earned corrections. Worse, he rises to the "challenge" of almost any large male dog that displays aggression/assertiveness (stares, hackles, growls, etc.) with gusto...basically he will leap into "battle" at any provocation. These fisticuffs (about 6 so far) have not resulted in any permanent damage to either participant, but we worry that this behavior SHOULD be corrected, and that if we ignore it, it may escalate to something worse. He has always played rough and most of his best "puppy friends" have been other large working dogs that similarly roughhouse.

The nature of the fights seem to be mainly "safe-ish", with lots of vocalization, open mouths, jumping up on hind legs, and head-head contact. Nonetheless, we fear that his willingness to scrap will get him (and us) into trouble before long.

DOGS ARE FROM NEPTUNE

While he occasionally acts in this manner while off leash, he (understandably?) behaves worse while on leash. When no dogs are about he is perfect, but he tears our arms off if he sees a dog, and he lunges, paws and growls when other dogs approach him on the leash. Self control is not his strong suit, and making him sit and relax only seems to "bottle up" the urge to be bad for a more dramatic release.

What should we do to try to reduce his urge to "mix it up" and how should we try to instill some tolerance into his fuzzy brain? We love him very much and are prepared to dedicate substantial time and resources to clear up this problem (despite calling him the miserable little toad when dragging him out of a mix-up).

Interesting problem.

The first thing to clarify is our rationale for intervening. Given Mufasa's stellar socialization history (nicely executed by you: bravo), there are trainers who might advise staying out of it, i.e. to let the environment do the training. The assumption is that nature knows what it is doing, that Mufasa's behavior, though distressing for the owners of the individual dogs in question (including yourselves), is normal and, by and large, safe, and a come-uppance and/or mellowing out with full social maturity will produce an acceptable solution.

My opinion is that it <u>is</u> worth toning down. The reasons are: his overwhelming manner will be genuinely stressful to some dogs, the come-uppance may be ugly if and when it comes and, most importantly, the potential primate public relations fiasco is considerable here (remember the two problems with dog-dog aggression: the dog behavior issues and the primate public relations issues). It would be terrible if he were ever unwelcome in the dog run which is reason enough for me to mess with it. Then, of course, there are also your torn-off arms from his lunging on leash.

For on leash walking, I recommend a Promise (Gentle Leader) halter to help you control the lunging. This is a great product, tailor-made for your problem and this particular brand fits brachycephalic breeds well. The big drawback is that he will act up the first few times you put it on, like a young horse. Make sure it is fitted correctly and stick to your guns - keep his early association with it as positive as you can (treats, praise). Dogs learn to accept their halters over time as they learn to associate them with walks. If you don't feel confident fitting or using a halter, look for a trainer near you who has experience with them.

Once he's used to wearing the halter, you can go to work on his on-leash manners. Can you arrange a few dogs a half dozen times to practise street passes? You need to find a combination of distance and repetition that will get your foot in the door, i.e. give you some rewardable responses early on. You will also have to set a reasonable standard. Initially, this might mean he gets rewarded for fighting the halter slightly less on the pass. Select from among the best responses he's giving you. Practise passing the same few dogs over and over. This will help it get a bit "old" as well as develop your eye for the range of responses he gives. Simply tell him "too bad!" and wrestle him past unceremoniously and matter of factly when he gives a poor response.

Keep in mind that your reward offering is going to have a hard time competing with the other dog in terms of attractiveness initially. So, to help level the playing field, work him when he's hungry (skip one or two meals) and use interesting and novel bait. Have at least two "tiers" of bait - coveted and even more coveted to refine quality control. The final goal is for him to do well "cold" on a new and interesting dog but this is grade 12 and he must start in grade 1. As he gets better with practice you can increase the level of difficulty by decreasing the distance, working him for shorter sessions (thus, reducing your reliance on warm-up), changing dogs and changing locations. This will bridge the gap to "real life" where you always get a novel dog, random distance and only one trial. The contrast between a dog at the beginning of such a training program (crazy out of control, won't take treats etc.) - it really looks like an impossible task - and after several troubleshooting sessions is remarkable.

DOGS ARE FROM NEPTUNE

For his off-leash bullying and fisticuffs, it's pretty apparent he's not getting much in the way of negative consequences from the other dogs. It is absolutely the case that there are dogs (Mufasa is the poster child) who are able to, given their size, athleticism and personality, lord it over virtually every other dog they meet and enjoy doing so. Call them "dominant." Call them "rambunctious" or "combative." Call them "bullies." The label is not important and can be distracting. What's important from a modification standpoint is that the behavior is going up in frequency and intensity and so is getting reinforced somehow. We would like it to go down. To do this we need to 1) get some control of the consequences, 2) decide what the standard is, i.e. define exactly what the illegal acts are around dogs and 3) develop a communication system to inform Mufasa precisely when he has done a glorious thing or committed an infraction (to bridge the lag between the infraction and the messy mechanics of collecting him for his consequence).

Here is how I suggest you proceed. Continue his regular off-leash exercise at dog runs. This is always, always, always the first line of defense for development and maintenance of social skills. First and foremost, notice and reward when he gets it right. It is suicide to ignore those "oh gee, I thought something might develop just then and it didn't..." moments. These are gold. Tell him he is Extremely Clever. If safe to do so (resource-guarding wise: watch food rewards in dog runs; if unsafe, stick with profuse praise), deliver to him a coveted food reward. This will become ever increasingly associated with the cooing which precedes it in this context. When I observe combative types in dog runs, what always strikes me the most are the missed opportunities - the times they get it right which go unnoticed and unrewarded.

The standard I suggest you set for giving consequences is failure to back off on first warning - from either you or another dog. In other words, being rambunctious is fine, rough consenting play is fine, defending himself if he's jumped is fine, even an attempt to harass is fine *if* the dog and you consent. If ever a dog threatens/warns/bites and he doesn't back off OR if you tell him to "don't touch the dog" or "drop the issue" or "that's enough please" or "come" (choose something that will roll easily off your tongue in the situation), he has a fork in the road. He can leave the dog alone and get the safety cue: "thank you" which means he has avoided the consequence that time. Or, he can ignore the warning, carry on and get the consequence, which you will signal, instantly (the very next move on a dog, post-warning) with "you're history!" or "you blew it" or "that's it! finished!" (again, choose what comes fast to your lips). Then, follow it up with the consequence.

The consequence must turn the knife in Mufasa's back, be worth avoiding. The broad choices are: aversives (pain/startle/fear) and reward/privilege removal. Your punishment will have to be big, explosive and dramatic to impact this strongly motivated behavior (small punishments - nagging - are usually worse than nothing at all). Most people don't have the stomach for this, and rightly so. There are also side effects to worry about. So that leaves us with reward removal.

You could put him on a cool-down down-stay on leash for a couple of minutes (don't agonize about this revving him up - it's a consequence, not a management attempt - if it elicits higher activity afterwards, that's his problem - he has many, many legal energy-burn off options and only one illegal move. Simply follow the system). You could give him a couple of minutes out of the dog run. You could march him home. You could do three-strikes-you're-out (first two boo-boos get him two minutes, third gets him marched home) or two-strikes-you're-out.

I would lean towards one or two strikes with this boy (either the first or second transgression wrecks it for him for that day). Just be sure you standardize it and apply it very coolly and unmercifully.

DOGS ARE FROM NEPTUNE

Dogs are great at flow charts. Here is yours:

BEHAVIOR	CONSEQUENCE
Standard play	continuing play
Turning the other cheek/not engaging in battle on his own	praise and possibly treat
Warning snap, snarl, growl or bite from a dog or warning cue from owner	*two choices for Mufasa*
Choice # 1 ceases and desists	"thank you" continuing play
Choice # 2 ignores warning & carries on	"you're history" + penalty

There is a partial management option here. You could get choosier about the times you enter the dog run, specifically avoiding adult males. The up side to this is fewer fights. The down side is Mufasa will be perpetually the biggest fish in the pond (a pretty minor consideration here as he is this anyway). And/or you could elect to avoid geris (decrepit sunset year dogs) and puppies who are most at risk from Mufasa's mow-'em-down interactions. The best solution might be a combo of management and flow chart. When the dog run looks do-able - not too many males so Mufasa will mainly play appropriately, no tiny puppies or feeble golden agers - go in and work the system. When it looks like it'll be too awful or risky, defer. Given your history, this part is optional. Whatever you do, don't avoid going altogether.

Lastly, it wouldn't be a bad idea to take up some sport with him. Lean towards mentally as well as physically challenging activities: tracking, search & rescue, competitive obedience, agility, free-style heeling are all good choices. You mention starting obedience. This is great.

P.S. boxers should be issued to their owners at age five <g>

DOG - DOG AGGRESSION

Growly in Class

I have a two and a half year-old intact male Irish setter, that gets along with all dogs except for a dog in agility class that was allowed to come running over and grope him before I was aware of the situation. The growling did not happen till later when this same dog made eye contact with him. My dog lives with five other setters, one of whom is another male, and we have had many dog visitors, and never had a problem with aggression.

The Promise collar has been suggested as a way to get my dog's attention in this class, but I fear that he will feel even more at risk from the other dog. I want him to be a therapy dog and don't like this precedent. Should I try to use the promise collar or just drop out of this class? I am a firm believer in each dog being allowed its space and was shocked that this poor dog etiquette from the other handler was allowed.

The fact that your dog has growled at another dog in his agility class in no way brings into question his suitability as a therapy dog. It is normal for well-socialized dogs to encounter individual animals who they do not like or are uncomfortable with and it sounds like this dog came on rather strong ("groping" - love that word - your dog). He is also reaching an age where he is socially mature and therefore more likely to behave assertively when his feathers get ruffled.

Your belief that every dog is entitled to his own space is very healthy. Some like more than others and this is fine. The way dogs maintain their space is with an array of body language and rituals. Things like dirty looks, growling, displaying teeth etc. are part of the communication system ("I don't like you this close, please go away"). There is a large school of thought that views any kind of aggressive behavior, however ritualized, as inappropriate and therefore grounds for reprimand or rehab. In the case of dog-human relations, I agree that any aggressive behavior needs to be addressed. But I think this is unwarranted for normal dog interactions, a perfect example of which is your dog letting this dog know with a growl that his approach is unwelcome.

DOGS ARE FROM NEPTUNE

You are already doing a good job of maintaining his social skills by virtue of the fact that he lives with four other dogs (okay, so the breed variety is lacking) and encounters regular visitors. If he plays regularly and you keep up these novel dog meetings, you have covered the foremost line of defense against him developing a problem vis à vis other dogs. It is not realistic to expect that he be enchanted by every dog he meets.

I don't personally see any reason to drop out of your agility class unless you are having a miserable time. It would indeed be better etiquette for the owner of the groper to keep him from harassing your boy. This is especially true if he is not reading the growl (i.e. backing off) or seems to want to have it out with him. If he is also an intact male, there is even greater potential for fisticuffs, which is no fun. Is there any untouchy way to enlist the help of this other owner? Dog people are notorious for resenting the implication that their dog is an instigator.

I like Promise halters very much though I'm not sure if one is called for here. You did not mention any lunging, pulling or pre-emptive striking on the part of your Irish and these are the behaviors the Promise collar really is effective for. One thing I would certainly do is be very heavy on the praise and baby-talk when your dog tolerates the presence or proximity of this other dog. Your tension is a vital ingredient to a recipe for increasing problems with this dog in the future. When he gets growly, try to distract him and switch his mood.

DOG - DOG AGGRESSION

Use of Food in Treating Aggression

I have a male Flat-Coat, Zeus, neutered. I also own a one year old St. Bernard (male, neutered). Roommates have a neutered male Aussie and spayed female Bullmastiff.

Zeus went through basic obedience at 6 months old (choke collar method). He did very well in training and is mostly off-leash.

He was always very dog and human friendly from day one. He let puppies climb on his head, played with every other dog. We went to the park often and played with many dogs in our complex. At that time, he was the only dog in the house.

Then I moved to the house with the Bullmastiff. Two months later, I purchased the St. Bernard puppy. Four months later, the Aussie arrived with roommates.

After the move, Zeus began to growl at some humans and has attacked several dogs (at the park, in Petsmart), usually puppies. The attacks look and sound vicious but are not prolonged and have never hurt any dog. He is tolerant of the Mastiff but will snap at him if he's pushed too much. Zeus and the Aussie love to play and wrestle together.

Zeus has also begun to growl more often at some humans. I can't see a pattern to the humans he doesn't like, but if they greet him with a friendly voice, he is usually very friendly and loving.

I have been told to keep him on leash to stop him marking off our property by two different trainers. I tried clicker training but abandoned it. One trainer recommended a high use of food treats for the rest of his training! I don't feel that is useful.

Do you have any suggestions how to get back my sweet ole dog?

Yes, there are a number of things you can do which have good track records at modifying both growliness with people and improving relations between dogs: shaping the absence,

DOGS ARE FROM NEPTUNE

counterconditioning, countercommanding and classical conditioning. Your results with these techniques will depend a great deal on your coming up with a powerful enough motivator to reinforce better responses as well as to pair with the stimuli you want Zeus to feel more comfortable about.

If your dog is addicted to a certain activity, such as fetch, Frisbee, tug etc. and will play relentlessly, never tiring, you're in business. High drive dogs offer us the luxury of a choice of potent motivators: aside from praise, food and avoidance, now we also have a game the dog will work very hard to get a dose of. It's why many serious trainers opt for these types of dogs, in spite of the price of living with one. They're maniacal but the payoff is more motivational options, good focus and stamina for training and a very intense, flashy quality to their work in most sports.

If your dog is not high-drive, you face a dilemma. The remaining dispensable motivators are praise, avoidance and food. As much as humans love indulging in the romance of it, praise is, for most dogs, a much weaker motivator than avoidance and food (and play). Don't get me wrong. I think it's important and I devote a great deal of energy trying to get people to praise their dogs more effectively. But, for the big jobs - reliable conditioning of behavior, distraction training, modifying fear and aggression - we haul out the heavy artillery.

In the case of obedience, there are definitely the other two options: avoidance and food. Both will get the job done if well executed, and the relative merits of each is an ongoing debate in dog training. For problems relating to fear and aggression, as is the case with your Flat-Coat, however, there is less choice. Although it is possible to suppress aggressive behaviors with punishment, there are fatal problems with going this route:

• The aversive must be strong enough to suppress deeply motivated behavior or to condition a competing response in the presence of elicitors for aggression. An aversive stimulus this severe is one which most people would be uncomfortable administering. It's bad for the health of whoever is training to

62

have to somehow reconcile to themselves hurting their "best friend" so severely, especially in light of non-aversive alternative techniques with better track records.

- The dog is put in a no-win situation on each trial: either tolerate the proximity of something that makes you uncomfortable (or perform the response that competes with fight/flight) or take the aversive. Trainers who employ aversives to suppress fear or aggression responses put dogs into these double binds on a daily basis. The cost to the dog in stress and health terms is both hefty and cumulative.

- From a classical conditioning standpoint, it is highly contraindicated to use aversives in the presence of something the dog is already not fond of. Now we are giving him another reason to dislike certain people or dogs: they predict an elevated likelihood of bad things happening to him.

You might make some headway with the Campbell "jolly routine" and some passive remedial socialization. These could be greatly enhanced and expanded upon if you chose to also use food. As is the case with many people, you're not wild about using food as a motivator. The prevalence of this sentiment is sufficiently widespread to merit some attention from those of us who are sold on the concept.

The principal objection to food training is rarely efficacy. There is no question that it works. Likewise, there are seldom arguments relating to invasiveness. It is safe and extremely forgiving of judgment and timing errors. The three most widespread arguments put forth against employing food as a motivator in training are:

1) wean off: that the trainer is locked into always having food available or else behavior falls apart,

2) distraction-proofing: that responses trained by positive reinforcement are less reliable in the presence of distractions than responses that are avoidance-trained and

3) corruption: that training with food cheapens the bond between dog and human, and/or ruins the dog's natural desire to please.

The wean-off argument doesn't fly. There are literally tons of data demonstrating the resilience to extinction of behavior trained with food reinforcement, not to mention a growing list of dogs achieving every training task attempted with exclusive use of food as reinforcer. It's that powerful.

I think the myth that food trained dogs always need to see food up front stems from a couple of accurate criticisms of *poorly executed* food training. The two classic food-training errors are:

1) not getting over the critical training obstacle of reinforcing responses with no reinforcer shown up front as elicitor (in other words, a poor job of prompt fading) and,

2) not putting acquired behaviors on some sort of variable reinforcement schedule.

But these are technical problems that are easy to solve and therefore an invalid indictment of food training per se.

The other chink in the wean-off argument armor is that, comparatively speaking, poorly executed wean-off of food reinforcement produces at least as good a result as poorly executed wean-off of aversive techniques. Dogs are very good discriminators, period. If the principal motivator is food and this is granted only when the dog has seen it up front, the dog will selectively respond when he sees food up front. He has learned that his chances are poor when he doesn't (a technical glitch that is easily remedied by reversing the contingency: selectively reinforcing when the dog does not see anything up front).

Likewise, if the principal motivator is avoidance which can be applied only when the dog is on a training collar, short of "breaking the dog" completely (punishing severely and frequently enough to obliterate most spontaneous behavior), the dog will selectively respond when leash and collar are on. In this case, the technical problem is often addressed with such things as long lines, and remote trainers primed with dummy collars to get off-leash response with no collar discrimination. The point is that poor administration of the technique will yield flawed results, regardless of whether you are into the carrot or the stick. If an incompetent, drunk surgeon kills someone on the operating table removing an appendix, the procedure "appendectomy" is not the problem.

The second reservation some trainers have about food training concerns its reliability. Sure, positive reinforcement is great, goes the argument, until heavy distraction comes along, then aversives must come to the rescue. As with wean-off, the reliability question is largely one of execution. How are the trainer's skills? What has been the progression of criteria-raises? In the case of "he doesn't like food" pleas, has the reinforcer been saturated or devalued by indiscriminate use? The reliability question could be appropriately raised in a case of severe, compulsive competing motivation and, even then, is still usually rendered one of personal training philosophy, i.e. which techniques is the trainer comfortable using (see Predation in the obedience section).

The final, and I think crucial, problem people have with food as a reinforcer is the feeling that the dog "should" perform without it. Once food is used to train, the Pandora's box is open, the dog has been corrupted, the bond between person and dog dirtied and the dream dies. What is this dream? It is the holdout fantasy that dogs want to please humans. We are their leaders and it should be a reinforcing event for them if we are pleased.

What always goes unspoken is that if dogs have an inherent desire to please us, then avoidance training - i.e. special collars - should also be unnecessary. What happens is the myth is protected and the *individual dog* is blamed if he requires additional motivating. This is where stubborn/willful/dominant come in. The myth itself is never scrutinized. The attitude of a non-conforming dog can be adjusted with some corrections, can't it? But this is simply using aversives to motivate. Liver would have also worked. So, why does liver cheapen the human-animal bond where pain does not?

DOGS ARE FROM NEPTUNE

I think the answer is that it is still possible to keep the wool over one's own eyes using avoidance to train. Praise, as the only positive reinforcement, can be fallaciously labeled as "sole" motivator. It is harder to do this when using food reinforcement. The trainer gets an instant dose of his place in the dog's motivational universe. A sudden explosion of focus and enthusiasm, even in low-drive dogs. I sometimes wonder if it works too well, prompting a "humph, why can't he work that way for ME?" backlash from the trainer. We've been indoctrinated to be "pack leader." Pack leader types, understandably, like feeling like #1 and the presence of bait can quickly make us feel bumped down in importance. It is too bitter a pill for some to swallow.

Those who merrily food train have made a critical leap in their thinking: their bond with the dog is separate from the technical task of manipulating his behavior. There is no rivalry. They don't see themselves in competition with the food for the dog's attention; they merely point out to the dog that they control his access to food. Ironically, they become a more powerful #1 than could ever have been achieved through intimidation. Some people find it magical to see the intensity for which a dog will work to eat - it is, after all, a very basic motivation. Others find it exclusionary. They feel out of the loop.

Put it this way: the dog has to eat anyway. No one will ever convince him that he doesn't love food. The choices are to either give it for free or exploit it for constructive ends.

If all this seems like I'm trying get you (and anybody else for that matter) to reconsider food training, you're right. I'm that sure of its usefulness.

DOG - DOG AGGRESSION

Bullying of Young and Submissive Dogs

I have a two-year-old Chessie who as a pup attended puppy class and has had quite a lot of socializing with other dogs. The problem is that about one year ago he started to go after younger and/or submissive dogs. He would scare them badly. I've also noticed that he displays this behavior when there is an object close by such as a ball, food (even dog dirt) or stick. He becomes extremely possessive and chases/growls/lunges at any dogs in the vicinity. I try to correct the behavior but unfortunately he is unleashed when it occurs and I can't always get him to come. Any ideas?

It's good that your dog is not injuring dogs but since he's scaring them and probably creating public relations difficulties for you vis à vis other owners, it would be nice to tone this down. Before getting into the nuts and bolts, I'd like to put the problem into perspective.

It really flies in the face of the human values of fairness, justice and compassion when dogs bully puppies and sweet little submissive dogs or get heavily possessive. They really seem to operate under a "Might Makes It Right" philosophy. And this is okay. It's their way. They're not us. If they had wanted or needed democratic institutions and laws to protect the weaker members of their society, they would have them by now. Luckily, like all successful animal species, they have evolved the capacity to aggress without fatal or maiming force.

Many people find dogfights extremely distressing to witness because it looks like "they're trying to kill each other" and speculate that they would have had it not been for the fortuitous intervention of nearby humans. By this logic, it must seem amazing that any animal species at all manages to not self-immolate, given that humans are never there to referee agonistic encounters. We also feel a strong need, after a dogfight, to assign blame. Who "started it?" Who was the bully? Who was victimized? This is not surprising, coming from the species that invented police, lawyers, religion and the taxonomy chart that puts

DOGS ARE FROM NEPTUNE

us at the pinnacle of evolution. We understandably get the urge to mete out punishment to perpetrators, compensation and protection to victims. It's our way. And this is okay too, as long as we recognize that we will have limited success cramming square pegged dogs into the round holes of human notions of justice.

The problem we have with their behavior is twofold actually: we take exception to the criteria they use for agonistic behavior because it is not like ours, and we also don't want any even minor injury or psychological blows sustained by any one individual dog at any time. Of course, this is not realistic; even with the well-developed ritualization that dogs have for their fisticuffs, there are rarely 100%'s in nature. Statistics dictate that a certain number of encounters will result in injury. And dogs, like wolves, do sometimes kill each other. Now this is far out at the skinny tail of the curve. The vast majority of dogfights are loud and blustery affairs that end in saliva encrustation or minor punctures and lacerations to the head, neck, back and shoulder areas. I'm in no way saying that we should not do everything in our power to minimize the likelihood of any dog ever getting hurt by another dog. I hate the idea as much as anyone does. I'm just saying we will best accomplish this minimization if we:

1) not waste too much energy on the small stuff,

2) not exacerbate the likelihood and severity of fights with some of our more ill-conceived interventions and

3) develop better prevention and treatment strategies than are industry standard at present.

Both of the scenarios you mention - harassment of puppies or submissive dogs and resource guarding against other dogs - are extremely normal behavior. Let's look at bullying

Many adolescent and young adult dogs, notably males, take up rolling puppies and bullying softer dogs, all in spite of fabulous play and socialization histories. The bad news is that it can make the target dogs really terrified of the bully, the bully's breed, his

68

type (e.g. "black dogs" or "big dogs") or, in the worst case scenario, dogs in general. The good news is it tends to be a developmentally limited issue: most bully dogs eventually outgrow the need to continually lord it over their peers.

If victim fearfulness *does* develop, it can manifest as flight/avoidance and sometimes as defensive type aggression or pre-emptive strikes. Problems are most likely to develop if the target dog has a shallow socialization history or is very young (obviously, genetic predisposition also plays a role but that is beyond the scope here). Dogs with lots of successful social contacts under their belts are at reduced risk when attacked and, if they develop fearfulness at all, tend to develop a more narrowly focused problem: the bully dog or the bully dog's breed or type, rather than dogs-in-general. This is why the cardinal rule of socialization is V&V: Volume and Variety. The more "padding" a dog has in the form of successful encounters, the lower the risk of a broad fear reaction when he has a bad experience.

The problem for you is that you don't have a crystal ball that will tell you which of your dog's targets are genetically predisposed and/or lack deep socialization. I feel strongly that, as far as socialization goes, it is the responsibility of owners to manipulate their own dog's social sphere to best advantage, including in the case of puppies and at-risk dogs, providing sufficient padding early on to maximize their dog's chances of coping with inevitable experiences like being targeted by another dog later.

Trainers get calls from accusatory people who feel their six month old's full blown dog phobia can be attributed to it being attacked by the dog down the street last week. On questioning, many of these dogs have had but a handful of minor - meeting and greeting on the street mostly - social contacts since being taken from their litters. Their fear is not the fault of the irresponsible owner down the street for letting their bully out. It is their own owners who utterly failed to prepare them for the world. A ton of padding can be in place by age six months. If there isn't, the dog is a sitting duck once something does happen. It's like engaging in six months worth of unsafe sex and then wanting to sue someone when you get AIDS.

DOGS ARE FROM NEPTUNE

That said, you can do a few things. Be sensitive to the composition at the dog park. While you will never be able to ID genetically sensitive dogs or dogs with no padding (if they made it to young adulthood and regularly go to a dog park, they have some padding), you can be prudent around really small puppies and take an educated guess about older puppies based on their breed or demeanor. You can avoid them or police/leash your dog when they are around.

You can also do what trainers like to do best: manipulate consequences and associations. If you are not already doing so, lay on the praise and baby talk when he interacts nicely or refrains from going on the assault, especially if the dog is a usual target-type. Hauling out food rewards might be risky, given his strong resource guarding. When he comes on too strong and you would like to penalize him, give it a name: "you're history!" and then follow up with the consequence. The "mark" will bridge the gap between the behavior and the consequence, exactly like conditioned reinforcers like clickers bridge the gap between desired behavior and primary reinforcers. For a consequence, I'd end his park privilege for the day. It will only take a few repetitions for him to learn that "you're history!" means it's over.

Many dog people advocate exposing bullies exclusively to large, assertive dogs who will "put them in their place." It might work but it might simply sharpen up his discrimination: which dogs he can and can't bully. Dogs have full social repertoires and are perfectly capable of being in the appeasement role in one encounter and rolling a dog in the next. There is also the risk of him developing fearfulness of certain dogs or types of dogs. Then you have problems on both ends.

For dog to dog resource guarding, the best policy is usually low intervention: stay out of it if they are not hurting each other. Dogs are very good at learning the warning signs that another dog has claimed possession. It is part of their culture. Some management would, again, be prudent: keep resources like food, balls, heavy affection etc. to a minimum in potentially contentious contexts.

70

With compulsive guarders, this won't completely get rid of it. Heavy resource-guarders like your dog will guard garbage, benches, people they happen to be standing next to, rocks, sticks, you name it. Sometimes you can de-fuse things by walking away, getting off the bench etc. and sometimes you can't.

If you are aware ahead of time of a likely guarding scenario - some focus like an interesting stick pulling a dog an area yours has already "claimed" - a safe strategy is to try and increase your or the other dog's distance from the object by distraction. The two ingredients for the possessiveness pie are 1) some coveted item and 2) more than one dog in proximity, often drawn in by the same magnet. Remove either of these ingredients and it fizzles out. If you can't manage to neutralize all resources, try to manipulate proximity.

Mood switching sometimes works (the "jolly routine," where you laugh at the dog when he gets all frowny and growly) if you have the discipline to giggle at very tense moments.

P.S. Remember to protect your recall command: *never* use "come" to get your mitts on the dog to "correct" him - you could end up with huge recall problems

DOGS ARE FROM NEPTUNE

Severe Attacks on Dogs

I teach a class to help with extreme dog aggression and in it I have a search and rescue trained two year-old female Belgian Malinois. She has tested to be high prey drive, high ball drive and fear aggressive. The testing was done by people who are supposed to know what they are doing, specializing in this sort of thing. She was spayed at 6 months and has lived with this same family since 8-10 weeks. They have a bloodhound and are knowledgeable dog trainers and owners.

It appears from the history that they have done everything right. She has been through several obedience and socialization classes before they came to me. I'm primarily a clicker trainer, doing mostly pet to competitive obedience training, agility and other fun stuff. She did eight weeks of a basic obedience-with-a clicker class, in which we paired the clicker with the reward of her Kong. She is not very food motivated. Her dog aggression was so bad she had to work in another ring from the class.

Rewards are given (thrown Kong and tug) for fewer stress behaviors, ignoring other dogs, less panting or spinning in circles here and at home. We have tried rescue remedy, St. John's wort and female hormones for several weeks, none of which have made any difference whatsoever that we could see. This dog will leave a stay or a trail to attack another dog.

I've tried an old spayed dachsie that honestly knows all the defusing signals (I use her a lot). She tried to kill her. I've tried puppies and she would kill them if given the opportunity. I tried my dog, who immediately gave up; the Malinois drew blood in several places. I was working in another ring once when she got away, came over the fence and attacked us from the rear. Her owner does the Alpha roll thing consistently as per the trainer before me taught her.

Today I had the owners leave the dog with me and go back to their home (two hours from me), as I wanted to see if the behavior was in any way connected to them. She has never been

*left before and was one devastated dog when they pulled out. I
immediately brought her to my office and loosed my tribe on her.
She was very frightened by an Airedale, Great Dane, Jack
Russell, three Scotties and a Chihuahua. I cued her to down and
stay, turned my back and started typing. Nothing: no growls no,
biting, nothing, nothing. Where do I go from here? Will this,
for instance, carry over to her owner???*

Major kudos to you and to her owners for persevering. Intense
aggression is difficult to treat - there is little sound information
generally accessible on how to proceed and it's a very long haul
sprinkled with incidents that are highly stressful for both owner and
trainer. The limiting factor is often peoples' patience. They just
can't take it anymore and give up.

In cases where people don't run out of gas, substantial improvement
is often possible. Plugging away is everything. Some people are
good at plodding and some are not. This is why client assessment
is so critical. Whereas in other dog training endeavors, there is a
plethora of techniques, most of which yield fast enough results for
even the most music-video patience level, in treating aggression
there are rarely fast fixes. Partly it's our responsibility as trainers to
prepare our clients for the long haul as well as support them
through the rough patches and partly it's a function of their history
and temperament: some people have it in them and some simply
don't.

Malinois are complicated pieces of machinery, combining that
extremely high drive with high reactivity and an impressive
offense-as-defense style. Some have terrific learning rates and
some are posts. They are not for the faint of heart. Here is how I
would proceed with this dog.

1) Detective Work: Why is this dog so upset around dogs? What
   are these owners doing to inadvertently feed the problem?
   What else is going on in her life? That she was so much better
   out of the presence of her owners is probably significant. It is
   also evidence that she is not too organically unglued, spinning
   in circles notwithstanding.

DOGS ARE FROM NEPTUNE

There is a lead here: the same trainers who indoctrinated alpha-rolling may have instilled other counterproductive habits. Calculate the probability of the dog receiving punishments - leash-jerks, reprimands, alpha-rolls, shakedowns, whatever - both in and out of the presence of other dogs. If it is significantly higher in the presence of dogs ("of course he gets punished a lot, he behaves so badly blah blah blah"), this is a critical piece of information which really needs to be addressed. It is hard to overstate the importance of reversing this trend.

A typical history of a dog like this contains some scrappiness early on, often in spite of decent socialization. It distresses the owners who become tense themselves around other dogs. As a result, they often limit social contact and begin applying punishments. Then it's pretty much downhill, especially when adolescence and adulthood kick in.

2) Desensitize her to wearing both a halter and a groomer's muzzle. The halter will be for on-leash work, the muzzle for off. In the case of the muzzle especially, introduce it carefully, with tons of positive associations. Muzzle on, attention, baby talk, treats. Muzzle off, ignore dog. Muzzle back on etc. Ration her food however much it takes to make her more food motivated as well as experimenting with kinds of bait. The more artillery we have, the better. Plus, tug will work on halter but not on muzzle, so we'll need food as a reinforcer any way you look at it.

The halter will pre-empt lunging to an extent, which will permit the owners to relax in class situations and on the street. Whenever she tries to attack another dog, they should laugh at her, manage it with the halter with as little emotion and drama as possible and then get her back on task. Zero aversives. Zero.

The muzzle will permit some free interaction without risk. Once she is sufficiently food deprived and thoroughly understands the clicker, I would selectively clicker train her around other dogs off leash. Early on, I'd make it excessively easy, with tons of rewards for just breathing. Later on, when she has made progress, there is the option of ending the session (and her opportunity for eating that day) abruptly for any attempted attack on another dog. You could initiate this yourself with the owners looking on from out of the room and then gradually introduce first their presence and then their participation.

3) They should do tons, I mean TONS, of "bar open - bar closed" type exercises: the abyss when there are no dogs around and a feast of treats, praise and tug when there are dogs present. This kind of associative learning gets at the underlying mood. It's slow (remember the bit about plodding?) but so worth it in the long run. They should pack special treats and a tug toy on all walks for this is where it is easiest to make the open and closed bar contrast. Dog approaching = bar open! Dog past = bar closed. Next dog = bar open! Etc.

Dogs who are selectively aggressive in their owners' presence may have had exactly the opposite sort of "bar" regime in their lives. Because the owners are so exasperated by their dog's behavior around dogs (not to mention badly advised), they mete out a lot of punishments and negative emotion at these times. They naturally, like any owners, wish they could act more lovingly and so might exhibit a "rebound lovingness" when dogs are not present. Also, the contrast in their dog is so great, it is easy to be baby-talking and rewarding. It feels to them like they are rewarding niceness in general when they attend to their well-behaved dog. Ironically, what they are in fact doing is opening the bar when dogs leave, exactly the opposite of what might turn around the dog around. The message the owners mean to send goes something like: "it's not YOU we hate, it's your behavior..." whereas this is translated by the dog as "the likelihood of affection and treats goes way up when dogs are gone."

So, she should be pointedly rewarded around dogs regardless of her behavior. The presence of dogs must predict good things. In the case of a sensitive dog like a Malinois, the owners' demeanor counts a lot: they must appear happy, relaxed, and baby-talky. If they don't feel it, they must learn to put it on until their confidence grows and it comes more naturally. This is not easy. And, they must close the bar when dogs are absent.

4) Stop employing alpha rolls and other aversives. This puts you in the unenviable position of having to contradict their previous instruction. One way to broach the topic is to point out that they have little to lose and that management is in place with the halter and muzzle. Also, bear in mind that punishment is a fast working technique. If it were going to work, it would have worked by now. If it isn't working, you're getting the side effects - association of the context with aversives - but not the cure. This is really, really not good.

5) Increase energy burning and problem-solving. Have the owners bump up the amount of work-to-eat, trick training, fetch and tug she gets on a daily basis. These kinds of routine interventions should impact her spinning in circles as well as the aggression.

These measures will produce a "dent" in the problem within six to eight weeks. Some dogs make faster progress but, even if they don't, a good resolution is still possible.

Nice Girls Do

If men are from Mars and women are from Venus, then dogs are from Neptune. I own a female Australian Cattle Dog who is almost two years old. In general, she gets along okay with other dogs but for some reason, has more than her share of friction with my friend's Border Collie female. They have both had decent socialization to other dogs throughout their lives and are nice dogs. We feel competent enough to manage it and they never hurt each other but we would sure love to know what's going on in their heads. There is no earthly reason for them to fight or have this personal animosity.

My friend's dog also used to be attacked a fair amount at flyball practice, both by another Border Collie and by a German Shepherd. It makes me wonder if she has some kind of bullseye on her. Any idea what might be going on?

It's important to always remind ourselves that we are in absolutely no position to judge whether a pair of dogs has "no reason" to fight or dislike each other. It would be like a committee of dogs deciding that humans had "no reason" to resent paying taxes. It's all just an exchange of worthless paper to them. There is a lot about dogs we do not fully understand and probably a lot going on between these two that we are missing.

We hold dogs up to unbelievable standards, standards we would never impose on humans. Imagine if we were supposed to love or even tolerate every single person we met, no matter how rude, hurtful or scary they were to us, or how much they pushed our buttons. And be nice at every encounter, no matter what kind of day we were having, no matter how we felt physically, no matter what the situation. And imagine if any or all our forms of accepted ritualized aggression - arguing, criticism, honking horns in traffic, letters to the editor, litigation, boxing – not to mention our outright aggressive legal acts like spanking kids, forcible detainment of "bad guys," retribution meted out by the justice system, sport hunting etc. – were considered aberrant behavior. It's ridiculous

DOGS ARE FROM NEPTUNE

yet we get very alarmed when dogs do the same kinds of things *their* way.

There is a myth among pet owners that "females fight less than males." Dog people know differently. While the highest likelihood of fisticuffs is between strange intact males, I would venture that, among dogs who know each other, female to female is the most common sparring combo. The front-runner explanations in your case are:

1) Resource guarding. Never underestimate the ability of a Cattle Dog or a Border Collie to zealously guard toys, bones, people, nearby air molecules etc. from other dogs. And in this case, *both* dogs are of the juiced up, high drive variety. Brrrrr!

2) Herding. One might be trying to herd the other, who resents the intrusion on her space and retaliates. How ironic. Remember, these are two breeds that are turned on by movement and that move a lot themselves, a perfect recipe for a vicious cycle (see the BCGSD syndrome, below).

3) Undersocialization. This is always a candidate when we consider the gap between what is the ideal amount of exposure and variety to keep social skills well lubricated and what most dogs get. It is doubly a candidate in the case of these harder-than-average-to-socialize breeds. We all think our dogs are well socialized until they get a little stiff, growly or fearful around some specific environmental element.

4) They just don't like each other for reasons we'll never relate to and that's okay. It's hard to like everybody. And when dogs don't like each other, this is how they behave. If you're a trainer type, you'll probably want to chip away (or blitz away) at modifying it but, if they're not damaging each other, this is optional.

You also allude to a neat thing called Border Collie German Shepherd Syndrome. I've seen it time and time again in groups of nicely socialized dogs that get along fine together. That is, until the

Border Collie gets turned on by something, gets all intense and goes after it. The German Shepherd gets turned on by the Border Collie, gets all intense and goes after the Border Collie. The Border Collie replies with the ubiquitous snappy "I'm BUSY right now" display, the German Shepherd sees the gauntlet thrown down and they start fighting. We see this at flyball practice a lot, until everyone gets trained to direct his or her focus to the task at hand.

It isn't always German Shepherds being turned by Border Collies. Other breeds can be in the formula and, of course, Border Collies get turned on by each other all the time with a rather pre-ordained result. Your friend's case is classic. This is sometimes misdiagnosed as redirected aggression.

Although I'm a proponent of accepting dogs as they are, including their – messy, uncalled for and off-putting to us – squabbling, I also think that we should often have a go at bringing it down a notch. For instance, when there are injuries, I believe strongly in intervening. We also have benign, dog-friendly techniques to intervene with and it is usually an improvement in everyone's quality of life when we succeed. Another bonus is the opportunity to learn more about dogs from our interventions and observations.

DOGS ARE FROM NEPTUNE

BEHAVIOR PROBLEMS

Counter Surfing

I have a yellow Lab, Buttercup, who is an accomplished counter surfer. She has nailed everything from loaves of bread to entire cartons of ice cream, consuming everything, including the carton. She once ate an entire box of Total Raisin Bran. How can I get her to stop?

I'll start by saying it's trickier to get rid of counter surfing in a dog who has had as many successes as your dog than it would be in a dog who has tried but never succeeded. It sounds like your dog has a nice, strong, intermittent reinforcement history for this behavior, the kind of history that makes behavior strong. We hate this.

Here are the options and the pluses and minuses of each. You can:

1) Extinguish ("starve") the behavior by arranging for her to have a zero success rate on lots of tries, until she stops trying.

- plusses: powerful technique, permanent result, and no nasty side effects

- minuses: hard to engineer perfectly (i.e. owner error-rate must be nil), dog may learn specific conditions where behavior is and is not successful (e.g. food placement on counter), technique does not bear instant fruit - attempts to make behavior pay off like it used to often get more intense before behavior dies and this is annoying for owners

2) replace the jumping behavior with one you can live with, for as good a reward (e.g., teach her to hold "stay" on a mat in the kitchen during food preparation time and reward her with tid-

bits at certain intervals: frequently in early training, less frequently as she gets more advanced at the exercise)

- plusses: fast-working technique if well-executed, no nasty side effects, solid stay as fringe benefit

- minuses: time-consuming for handler in early training when rewards are at frequent intervals, handler must be alert especially in early training as dog must be given a No-Reward-Mark at instant of break, does not necessarily solve owner-out-of-room type jumping problems

3) dog proof when you're not around and, when you are available, do set-ups ("stings") so you can interrupt and redirect

- plusses: teaches what you **do** want in a clear fashion, makes you consider how attractive the alternatives are (i.e. does your dog have interesting toys, ways of winning food prizes etc.?)

- minuses: may not touch owner-absent jumping, requires decent timing skills from owner,

4) punish her into oblivion with a "remote trainer," i.e. shock collar at the instant her feet come off the ground

- plusses: fast suppression of behavior if well executed and if every instance caught

- minuses: inhumane and harsh, especially considering the "crime," dog may learn to discriminate when collar is on or off and/or owner around to press button, requires perfect timing, possible nasty side effects of using pain

5) punish her into oblivion interactively, e.g., yelling, screaming, scruff-shake, alpha roll, smack dog with 2 x 4 etc.

- plusses: hmmmmm, none I can think of

- minuses: erosion of dog-owner relationship, possibility of pain or fear-elicited aggression, likely discrimination learning: owner around = punishment, owner not around = no punishment, temporary effect, if any, hand-shyness, ruining a perfectly good 2 x 4 on the titanium-like skull of a Labrador

6) punish her with a "scat mat" or other booby-trap like device

- plusses: good timing of punishment if well executed

- minuses: possible discrimination learning between booby-trap/scat mat present or absent (i.e. behavior safe to do when the above are absent), possible acquired phobia of innocuous elements present at time of aversive (e.g., fear of cans if empty cans used), takes skill to rig good booby-trap, must catch every instance of behavior, side-effects of employing pain

My recommendation would be a combination of extinguishing the behavior when you're not around and teaching the alternative down-stay when you're doing food-preparation. This means you will have to dog-proof like crazy for a while when you're not supervising. Learn her "reach" and always keep goodies beyond it. It also means some practice at down-stay both separately and for a few meal preparation times.

Catch any attempt to leave the mat with a No-Reward-Mark ("AH!AH!"), replace the dog in the stay and reward good stays at unpredictable but frequent intervals. After a few sessions you can graaaaadually stretch the intervals out, culminating in a dog that will hold her stay for the entire time you prepare the meal for her treat at the end.

You could supplement this with a couple of cooked up sting operations. Sometimes this speeds up the extinction process. Make sure your dog has attractive stuffed toys to unpack on a regular basis. This kind of problem-solving to obtain food is one you can live with.

DOGS ARE FROM NEPTUNE

Apartment Barking

I am on the verge of being evicted from my apartment because of my dog's incessant barking. Shrapnel is a one year old Maltese from a reputable breeder. I deliberately avoided buying a miniature schnauzer or sheltie because of their barky reputations and now I feel like I am no further ahead.

He is fine when I leave and fine with the doorbell, just a few barks and then he is happy to greet the visitors. The problem is the morning and when he wants my attention. He wakes up at five a.m. or earlier and, if I don't get up and play with him or take him for a walk, he barks until I do. I stay in bed and pretend to be asleep as long as possible to see if he will give up but he is very stubborn. If I try going to bed earlier the night before to compensate for my lack of sleep in the morning, he just wakes up even earlier! He is deafeningly loud and the neighbors are not amused. This week I received notice that he is a nuisance and I will either have to get rid of him or else move.

He also barks when I am home and ignoring him by working or talking on the phone. I have to pay attention to him to make him knock it off. I have tried ignoring him and the barking got worse. I tried increasing his exercise - he goes to the dog park almost every day - and obedience classes, but it made no difference. In desperation, I got a citronella collar and, although he seemed to hate the smell, he kept right on barking so I returned it for a partial refund after a couple of days. If I don't find a solution, I will have to place him because, even if I move, it would have to be to another apartment. This would break my heart because I love him and he is perfect otherwise. Someone suggested I put a shock collar on him or have his vocal cords cut but I don't relish either of those options. Is there anything else I can try?

Puppies are programmed to make distress calls when they find themselves alone. When the bitch hears the distress call, she locates the puppy and retrieves it to the litter. So, there is a hard-wired component to dogs making noise when they are alone or wanting attention. Dogs can also learn to bark to get what they want, just as they can learn other behaviors through operant conditioning. When they want something, they experiment with their behavior and learn, through trial and error, what works. When they make noise and the crate opens, owners attend to them and walks are initiated, they settle on barking as a strategy.

Owners are fascinated with the communication aspect: "he's TELLING me he needs to go out" and leap to fulfill the dog's apparent request. It could very well be that the dog would like the door opened at that second. What's important is **how** he is trying to get what he wants. Bottom line: if you don't like the behavior, don't reward it. Wait for something better and *then* give the dog what he wants.

In your case, there is a strong learned component: from Shrapnel's perspective, barking sure works, doesn't it? The technique of choice in this case is extinction: ignore barking and only grant him what he wants - attention and outings - when he has given up and is waiting quietly. There are two flies in the ointment in your case:

1) You have inadvertently conditioned nice, strong, resilient-to-extinction barking by waiting as long as possible in the morning before cracking and getting up, and

2) Your partial attempt at ignoring him, which failed.

I'll explain what I mean.

When behavior is maintained by reinforcement and you want to get rid of it, withholding the reinforcer is called extinction. The behavior dies because it no longer works. How quickly and easily the behavior dies is largely a function of what sort of reinforcement schedule it is being maintained on. A reinforcement schedule is simply the frequency of reinforcement. If you work for a company, you probably receive reinforcement - your paycheck - every two weeks. This is an example of a fixed interval schedule (FI). The interval is fixed: every two weeks. Reinforcement can also be doled out by unit of work: instead of paying you every two weeks, you are paid for every ten things you produce, regardless of how long it takes you. This is a fixed ratio schedule (FR). The ratio is fixed: every ten units.

Behavior can remain alive and kicking on quite thin (infrequent) reinforcement schedules, if training is well executed. We'll produce hundreds of units or hours of behavior to get reinforced under the right conditions. Every type of reinforcement schedule has features associated with it. The feature that concerns you is resilience to extinction.

Interval and ratio schedules can also be variable. Instead of being rewarded every two weeks (14 days), you are rewarded every two weeks *on average*. This means that sometimes the paycheck comes after 12 days, sometimes after 16, sometimes after 19, sometimes after 8 etc. It averages out to every 14 days but you never know exactly when the paycheck is coming. Variable ratio schedules work the same way.

You can also be rewarded continuously: you get paid for every single instance of the behavior. Every time the dog sits, he is rewarded versus being rewarded every five sits (FR), after five minutes of practicing sit (FI), after every five sits on average (VR) or after an average of five minutes of sit practice (VI). When teaching new things, continuous reinforcement works best. Once behavior is already learned (plateau'd out in frequency), it is better to stop rewarding continuously and to adopt one of these (or other) schedules to maintain it.

When I say "better" I mean "more resilient to extinction." Behavior is at greatest risk of extinction if it has been rewarded continuously. It is much "tougher" if it has been rewarded intermittently. The greatest resilience of all comes from a thin, variable schedule. Think of it this way. If you are used to getting rewarded after every unit you produce, or every couple of seconds, you will definitely notice the difference when the rewards stop coming. If, on the other hand, you are used to being rewarded on a thin variable schedule - sometimes after a month, sometimes after three, sometimes after five and half weeks etc., it will take longer for you to notice that rewards have stopped. The dry spell feels like it could be part of the schedule.

What has happened with Shrapnel is that, when you tried waiting him out in the morning, he got used to having to produce a lot of behavior on a variable interval schedule. This toughened up the barking enough so that, when you tried ignoring him, the behavior didn't die quickly. The "getting worse" (called an "extinction burst") you observed was, ironically, a sign that extinction was nearly over, kind of a final rattle of the behavior before it dies. Then, when you cracked, an even thinner schedule got stamped in, not to mention the more intense version of the barking. He learned that if at first you don't succeed, keep trying; you'll be rewarded eventually.

Another catch is the fact that you are an apartment dweller. Pressure from the environment forces you to crack before extinction kicks in. You're trapped into worsening your problem. So, you have two ways to go:

1) Beg the neighbors' and landlord's indulgence and extinguish it once and for all. Think of it as short-term pain for long term gain. If you go this route, it is absolutely imperative that you stand your ground and, no matter what, never attend to him or otherwise reward his barking. Hold out to the bitter end. Keep in mind that it will get worse before it gets better. Don't crack.

    You may be able to buy yourself a faster extinction by rewarding continuously for a while before commencing the "kill." For a couple of weeks, immediately spring out of bed whenever he begins barking and, when you're home, instantly reward any barking with attention or whatever else he is after. You're setting the behavior up for a fall. When you start the extinction schedule, the contrast will be greater.

2) Have another go with the citronella collar. If he "hated" the smell, it will probably work eventually. The citronella collar works by punishing barking on every trial. What we know about punishment is that, if it is going to work, it will do so in

the first few trials. Citronella collars, by contrast, often take two or three weeks to substantially reduce barking, which seems to contradict this rule about punishment. My suspicion is that citronella collars are an example of extremely *un*prepared learning. Animals are wired up to form certain kinds of associations more easily than others. It is easier for a pigeon to learn to peck for food rewards than it is to avoid shock, easy for certain species of monkey to learn to avoid snakes than to avoid other features in their environment etc. This is referred to as "prepared learning," i.e. genetically prepared. Reproductive advantage is conferred on individuals who more quickly learned certain things. I don't think dogs are wired up to easily form associations between their barking and unpleasant odors.

Dogs wearing citronella collars seem to form all kinds of superstitious associations before their barking emerges as common denominator. They avoid certain locations where the collar went off, certain people or dogs, sniff expectantly when they hear a doorbell sound etc. With enough trials, it is as though they have the realization "Oh! It's my *barking* that makes the smell, I get it now!!" and the problem is solved.

As much as I dislike punishment, if it turns out your neighbors or landlord will not grant you a training grace period, the citronella collar is a better solution than placing your dog.

Mouthiness during Play

We adopted a two-year-old, recently neutered, shepherd cross from the pound four weeks ago. He was a stray, so we don't know anything about his background. He is basically a very friendly, sweet animal.

We play "fetch" and "tag," but no tug-of-war games. If he gets possessive over a toy, I take it away and the play session is through for the day. He also gets plenty of exercise (long walks, as well as the play sessions). He has never growled or anything like that. In fact, he will let me remove his food dish while he is eating, no problems.

The problem we do have is that he doesn't seem to know how to "play nice." He grabs with his mouth and clamps down hard. He has broken the skin on me three times and left many, many, MANY colorful bruises. I am especially worried about this behavior with my six-year-old. I *know* he only means to play, but these HURT!

I have tried telling him "NO BITE." I have tried yelping (the best I know how, not sure how it should sound) and then ignoring him. I have tried correcting him with a training collar. Nothing seems to work.

Do you have any advice?

I'm glad you're being conscientious about addressing this rough play. The bites you describe are unacceptably hard and would be even more serious directed at your six-year-old.

You are on the right track insofar as you are providing outlets for his energy and searching for a consequence to supply for his mouthiness during play. A couple of things come to mind that may help account for the lack of progress. It might be that one or other of the consequences you have tried had some impact on him but, because improvement didn't kick in right away, you switched strategies. Toning down rough play (without blowing the dog away with extremely harsh punishments) usually takes some repetition. It is a deeply motivated and self-reinforcing behavior. It is also possible that he has found your consequences to date a little lightweight or is unsure what aspect of his behavior is the problem.

The consequence of choice for rough play is time-out - a two-minute social isolation penalty. The reason it is such an effective consequence for this behavior is that it removes exactly what the dog wants most in the world at that second: interaction with you. It also avoids the violence-escalation risk and side effects that go along with physical punishments. When people announce that they tried time out and it "didn't work," usually it means one of two things: their execution needs fine-tuning or else they did not do it at all or were inconsistent. Without a clear trend, consequence-wise, the behavior does not get modified.

The ideal time-out has a few requirements:

1) It must truly be a negative consequence for the dog or there is no incentive to avoid it in future. "Ignoring" the dog while he continues to chomp on your leg, holding up a kid while the dog leaps around trying to grab clothing, putting the dog into the bathroom where he has a wonderful time shredding toilet paper and eating soap, leaving the room only to have him target someone else who is still present - are all examples of completely ineffective time-outs.

It is imperative to use a barren room, pen or crate. People get very antsy about the crate suggestion as they have been indoctrinated to not associate the crate with punishment lest the dog come to hate his crate. This is unnecessarily rigid. The punishment is the removal of opportunity to interact, not being in the crate per se. If, for instance, you were hanging out together with the dog IN his crate, having an enjoyable time wrestling, cuddling or holding a bone for him to chew on and the dog misfired with his jaws, you may very well boot him

OUT of the crate as consequence. Would the dog then associate being out of the crate with punishment? There are serious logical flaws in the "oh, never put the dog in the crate as punishment..." refrain.

What's important is that you can orchestrate an effective time-out by pointedly removing any possibility of the dog interacting with you or having any fun. The mechanics of accomplishing this are moot.

2) The time-out must be clearly signaled. However you choose to supply the time out, there will be some inevitable lag between the dog's transgression and the consequence. To sharpen up the association, you will give some clear signal that the dog has crossed the line at the instant he gets too rough. Typical "marks" are "OUCH!!," "Too bad!" and "You're history!" The dog will learn, through repeated experience, that the mark predicts the time out and will serve to pinpoint the **exact** moment the dog screwed up.

3) There must be a clear and do-able standard. A common problem with time-outs is lack of clarity about the threshold the dog must not cross. Typically, people provide the time-out when they lose their patience instead of in response to a certain level of jaw pressure. If play ends at a certain degree of mouthiness which, on other occasions, was tolerated, progress will be slow or non-existent. The time-out is not about informing the dog that you are angry: it's about drawing an objective line in the sand. The message to the dog is that X-degree of jaw pressure on humans abruptly ends interaction. This gives the dog clear choices.

At the end of the two-minute penalty, resume interaction with no grudges. If he does it again, he gets another time-out. If he does a few in a row, consider giving him a "game misconduct" penalty: end play permanently for that day. With this regime in place, look for a measurable reduction in the incidence and intensity of his mouthing in two to three weeks. A dog halter could also be incorporated if you have difficulty managing him, i.e. escorting him to the penalty box.

You may also want to further beef up the Raptor's exercise and problem solving to help the cause. Add hide & seek (for toys or for people) to your game repertoire, teach him tricks or obedience to give him some mental challenge, make him work for part or all of his food ration by stuffing chew toys, using it as rewards during training and hiding it around the house. There are also organized dog sports like agility, flyball, free-style and obedience. It is a rare dog who has too much work to do.

The raptor would probably also benefit from an obedience course. These courses are nothing like the drudgery they used to be years ago: the methods are more sophisticated and are both dog and people friendly. The Association of Pet Dog Trainers (1-800-PET-DOGS) may be able to refer you to a trainer in your city. Choose a course where your child can be somewhat involved in the training. Kids need leverage over dogs and well-executed obedience training is a great way to achieve this.

Garbage Raiding

We have a rescue Kelpie, of undetermined age (but with pretty advanced PRA, so probably about six or seven years old) that lived on the streets for some time before he could be captured by Kelpie Rescue.

He's a very good dog in most respects, but just can't resist tipping over all the wastebaskets when we're not home. He eats whatever he finds, including extremely unappetizing objects.

We try to always close the bathroom doors and put the kitchen trash out of reach when we leave. We don't always remember. Also, recently when we installed doggie doors through the garage to the back yard, we spent a week dog-proofing the garage, finding new things he could get into each day upon returning home. Soap! Yum. I think he may have thumbs that he hides somewhere. I understand that punishing him when we come home is useless (although he has perfected a lovely grovel). Large amounts of cayenne pepper in the trash didn't slow him down for an instant. I haven't invested in mousetraps yet, but that's the only other suggestion I've heard.

Because he has had extensive training in the positive value of getting into the trash, we understand it would take even more extensive training to get rid of this established behavior pattern. He's quite wary, and doesn't often try any garbage moves when we're around. Would it be worth trying to stop this behavior, or should we just keep training ourselves to put the trash out of his reach?

I've always been impressed by what dogs will eat. Their merry ingestion of plastic wrap, soap, tissue, cardboard, wood, feces and rocks etc. is one of many reminders that they are not us. What we would like, of course, is for them to readily eat what we present to them and forego all else. Dogs are so opportunistic, however, that this rarely happens by itself. They are programmed to not hesitate if they get a chance at garbage or, better yet, part of your lunch. We call it a "behavior problem." They call it "eating." They are great explorers, have a well-developed regurgitation reflex that will kick in if necessary and, barring specific disease, relatively ironclad digestion so they are well endowed for the scavenging lifestyle. They are also pretty good troopers when it comes to circumventing adversity in order to succeed. In other words, mousetraps and hot pepper are usually just obstacles to work around.

As you point out, Tommy has a successful history, from both his street life - where his scavenging skills were honed - and his life with you so far. So, yes, you're up against Strong Behavior. What I suggest is a combination of:

1) extinction of garbage-targeting and

2) providing another type of scavenging activity to burn the energy he has learned to save up for your absences. This will buy you time to:

3) teach him some problem-solving activities for edible payoff that he can engage in when you are at home - if you can thus rearrange his schedule, he will start to click the "off" switch when you leave rather than when you are at home, in order to save up his scavenging juice for the games.

Extinction is killing behavior by not providing reinforcement. It is an extremely underused tool (it is also an extremely misused term, often mistakenly substituted for the word punishment - you don't "extinguish" behavior by providing yucky consequences, you extinguish behavior by providing dull consequences). The best way to go about this is to deliberately leave out wastebaskets with fake garbage, i.e. nothing of interest to Jack, every day. You may need to do trial runs to discover what constitutes non-reinforcement for him. For your **real** trash, have another couple of bins that are carefully locked out of reach. During the training period, make a real effort at getting this right *every time*. The ideal thing is for him to try and fail, try and fail, try and fail. There's never any good stuff in those wastebaskets anymore. Boooooring.

At the same time, you will provide an alternative "legal" scavenging activity for absences. Leave small cookie bits in out-of-the-way corners all over the house, garage and yard as well as a few bigger prizes: "carcasses." A good Kelpie-level carcass would be a tightly stuffed Kong toy or marrow bone, wrapped tightly in a cloth diaper or other expendable tough fabric, sealed in an old margarine type container and hidden in a spot that's hard to locate and/or hard to access. Make him work.

Now, he has to know it exists so you must start off with easier hiding places and a cookie on top (or even a trail leading to it) to get him started the first few times. You can also stuff the Kongs more loosely and with smaller bits, tie the rag loosely and fail to seal the container completely to make it easier. After a few successes, start tightening things up. Challenge is the point. Also, teach him that the ritual of the stuffing, wrapping and sealing followed by dogs being locked up while you randomly scatter cookies and hide the carcasses predicts you leaving for work and his scavenging opportunity. The build-up will help. It is likely that he has been doing his best work shortly after you leave.

Vary the stuffing in the Kong fairly regularly and reduce his meal ration accordingly. You may also have to reduce your other dogs' rations if they are cashing in on the new regime (their expected participation is another reason for providing more than one carcass - and don't agonize if he or another dog gets more than their share). I have had clients who got so hooked on the "work to " routine that they threw away their food dish. They also ended up with extremely few behavior problems and happy, well-adjusted dogs.

A long enough period of well-executed dog-proofing combined with an interesting legal alternative is a final solution in many cases. If you'd like to eventually be able to slack off a bit on the garbage hiding, however, I suggest you also re-arrange his clock so his "on" switch is triggered by specific games and not by you leaving the house. To accomplish this, you must come up with some games that fit the bill. In the case of a high drive dog, the best are fetch (if his vision permits) and tug. In Tommy's case, I would also suggest some sort of problem-solving activity for food rewards (again, reduce his "free" food accordingly).

The important rules of engagement for tug of war are:

1) Designated Toy and Start Command: the game is only played with one specific toy and never with anything else, and there is a specific initiation command

2) Dog Must "Out" On Command: out-on-command (taught with food rewards) gets the game re-initiated, whereas failing to out causes a time-penalty or, if severe, a game misconduct (game ends)

3) Frequent "Obedience Breaks" in the Action: these are "outs" followed by a bit of obedience (sit-down-tricks) followed by re-initiation as reward

4) No Uninvited Takes: dog must not grab before the initiation command or else face a time-penalty or game misconduct

5) Jaw Prudence: dog must never accidentally knick you or he faces a game-misconduct. Even if you deliberately "feed" Tommy your hand, he must go out of his way to avoid it. **No exceptions**.

There are a few problem-solving-for-food options for Tommy. One is clicker training. Once he's conditioned to the clicker, shape tricks or simple movements for a little while each day. This is a terrific and convenient way to promote mental fatigue. It is much better to put a lot of your eggs in the mental fatigue basket as opposed to going strictly with a regime of hard physical exercise. Many people with destructive dogs initiate impressive exercise programs - a couple of hours of roadwork per day etc. This takes the edge off the behavior problem but one ends up with a dog who is still understimulated vis à vis exploratory behavior and problem solving, only now he is a conditioned athlete. Aaaaiiiieee!!!

Another is to play hide and seek for cookies, treats or kibble. You can phase in rounds of cookie-searches while you're home as you phase down cookie-searches when you're away. You can also play hide and seek for the tug/fetch toy. Another idea is to give him a job or two to do, preferably involving putting things in his mouth. Teach him to fetch items by name, help you put away the laundry (one of my dogs puts the socks in the sock drawer) or tidy up the yard, always for food rewards. Every little bit helps the understimulation cause. As he discovers that these strategies obtain much, much more interesting ingestibles than garbage raiding, and that he can rely on regular opportunities to win them, his motivation to go for trash receptacles will dissipate. Dogs do whatever works.

DOGS ARE FROM NEPTUNE

Elimination on Sofas

A person on the Internet suggested I ask you this, so here it is:

A man called me for advice about a 10 month-old neutered male Boston Terrier. He (the dog <G>) is well housebroken. Recently, while the guy was at work, the dog got out of his crate, got up on the only two forbidden surfaces in the house, the bed and the sofa, and peed and pooped on each. He has repeated the behavior several times since, while the man was home and nearby but not watching closely.

Of course he told me the dog resents being left alone and is eliminating out of revenge, etc. I know this isn't true, but why do dogs sometimes go on beds or bed-like surfaces? I know they prefer absorbent surfaces, but the carpet is absorbent. Why a place where the dog really wants to be? The guy says the dog always wants to get up on these places when they are together, and they are the only places that are off-limits. The dog is pleasant in other respects, gentle and amusing, not pushy. What do you think?

Dog trainers hate it when this happens. We painstakingly attempt to indoctrinate our clients about behavioral principles, some basic canid ethology and steer them away from the spite-revenge-plotting-military-coup motives they so often ascribe to their dogs. Then the thing pees on the sofa. Makes you want to become a pastry chef.

For the record, I really don't think dogs view the products of their elimination as despised trump cards in revenge operas. They are not capable of forming a representation of another being's future punishment by an action they engage in now. Plus, they think urine and feces are quite fascinating.

There are a few things to rule out before entertaining the revenge theory. One is that some dogs, aside from having natural preferences for absorbent urination substrates, have other idiosyncracies about elimination. Given a choice, many like to

98

defecate into bushes or long grass, are more inclined to both urinate and defecate along fence or other boundary lines, get the urge to urinate in streams or shallow water, and like being on slopes or "high ground" for one or both functions. One possible explanation or partial explanation for the Boston is that he is a high-ground enthusiast. If he's full and encounters a nice high, porous area, possibly earthy-smelling area (how many dog trainers hear tales of dogs leaping on beds post-human-sex and peeing...), he is stimulated to eliminate. It worked the first time - relief is pretty reinforcing - so a habit was born.

If these areas had been forbidden, it would delay the owner finding out about his dog's penchant as well as setting the stage for the ubiquitous revenge speculation. And, yes, it's possible that he really wanted to be there when the owner was there for one set of reasons (near owner, comfort etc.) and, when he finally did get there got the urge to eliminate.

A longer shot worth knocking around is the idea that the dog was excited to be cruising around out of his crate at a time of day he normally wasn't exercising and doubly excited to be able to leap up onto novel areas that had previously proven dangerous. The excitement loosened him up and this, possibly combined with the high surfaces and novelty made him likely to let fly. It was reinforcing enough to be worth repeating, obviously. There's also an *extremely* outside case for separation anxiety as a trigger for the initial incident.

In the more likely division are a couple of other notions: that the dog was not "well housebroken" to start with (by definition we can run with this) and the reliability of the reported facts. Never underestimate the (unconscious) ability of people to arrange the facts in a way that suits their current needs or the needs of the story they are telling. We all do this at times. This guy may need, for a bunch or reasons (the front-runners here are usually "see what I have to put up with?" "my problem is NOT garden variety!" and "NOW can I rub his nose in it?") to have a "housebroken" dog "suddenly" break training and go in the "only two" forbidden places in the universe exactly as a response to resentment. It's a case of having a pet theory first and squeezing the facts into it rather than using facts to build a theory. For instance, what is this dog's **real** accident history? How was he originally housetrained? Did the owner empty the dog that morning before leaving him alone? How is it the dog has managed to repeat the same mistake "several times since" the owner has had the wake-up call that his dog is not trained? I would think a dog eliminating on my furniture would make me supervise pretty closely, crate when my back was turned and re-institute a reinforcement-for-outdoor-elimination regime.

BEHAVIOR PROBLEMS

Mounting

I have a two-year-old chocolate lab named Maggie. In the last couple of months, she has discovered a behavior that less than pleases me, but I am not sure how to handle it.

When playing with other dogs, she has started mounting them. Male, female - it doesn't matter. They wrestle for a while, and before I know it, there she goes humping away! I try calling her, but she doesn't come (her recall is otherwise very good). If I pull her off and say NO! BAD DOG, she stops for a few seconds and then goes right back.

In all other respects she is very non-dominant (a little on the submissive side, if anything). I am sure this is a learned behavior, but how do I get her to stop?

I understand your squeamishness about mounting. It's a behavior that many people are uncomfortable. I also take your point that it compromises your recall. There are a few things that may help you in your predicament.

Firstly, recognize that, in the context you describe, there may not be any social significance to her mounting other dogs. In other words, there isn't always a "big" reason for motor patterns performed out of context. It is unlikely that she is trying to have sex with or express dominance towards these other dogs (as armchair ethologists in the park have probably suggested). She is excited, having a good time and out pops the behavior. No harbinger of bad news vis a vis her temperament, hormones or social skills necessarily.

This also makes it easier game for modification, which is what you're after. You have a few choices, modification-wise. You can try any combination of redirection (counter-commanding), punishment, shaping the absence or putting it on cue.

Redirection is getting her to "switch gears" to a mutually exclusive behavior when she gets in the mood. By now you probably have an

101

DOGS ARE FROM NEPTUNE

idea of the precursors: a certain time interval spent wrestling, perhaps a certain style to the wrestling, perhaps certain dogs, anything that tips you off that mounting is imminent. Before she mounts, obtain and reward another behavior, the gear-switcher. Try calling her (your chances are better pre- as opposed to mid-mount) and doing a two or three trick sequence for a really coveted, rarely given reward. Then send her back to play, always vigilant to interrupt if she seems to be winding up again. You will eventually be able to relax your supervision when she starts self-recalling at those times (anticipation is a wondrous thing sometimes).

Punishment is supplying a consequence after she starts. I don't recommend aversives but would entertain reward removal: "you're history, rude dog!" and escort her from the dog area for a couple of minutes' penalty as soon as she starts. You could have a "three strikes and you're out" rule, i.e. march her home on the third penalty she receives on any given day. Dogs are very good at learning these kinds of contingencies. This is a beefier consequence than the one you've already tried (verbal reprimand).

Shaping the absence is an under-used and powerful technique. It is simply noticing and rewarding Maggie when she *doesn't* mount, given opportunity. We are all guilty of ignoring some of the best behavior in our dogs. What's tricky about shaping the absence is the psychological hurdle for the trainer: that the dog won't immediately "know" what the reward is for. In fact, it is not necessary for any subject to "know" the reason for in order for conditioning to take place. God, I love dog training.

Sometimes it will look like you are rewarding her for playing with a dog (without mounting), sometimes it will look like you are rewarding her for disengaging in playing with a dog (without mounting), sometimes it will look like you are rewarding her for switching to playing with another dog (without mounting), sometimes it will look like you are rewarding her for ignoring a dog (without mounting), for checking in with you (without mounting), for telling off a dog (without mounting) etc. There is one common denominator (without mounting). The power of trend. No instant pudding but huge dents in behavior over time.

Put it this way: you're going to the park anyway; may as well reward non-instances for the heck of it.

Mounting is one of those behaviors that goes nicely onto a cue. If you can classically condition her mounting to a verbal command and follow up the commanded mounts with extrinsic rewards (and follow up the non-commanded mounts with nothing or even reward removal if you are combining techniques), you are on to something. Control. What dog trainers love best. It's almost as though the new cue - your command - takes over as trigger from the old cue - intense wrestling.

This is meeting the dog halfway. "Okay, I recognize you enjoy mounting, but please do it only when I tell you to" is a deal dogs find easier to live with than "never do this enjoyable behavior." Deal-cutting or channeling also works well with compulsive predatory behavior (El Diablo, the Border Collie on the cover, attacks the vacuum only when told and after a period of quietly waiting, poised - she is penalized with a delayed attack command consequence for premature attacks) and with pulling on leash: "walk nicely for X distance in order to get the 'mush' command".

To condition, instead of redirecting when you notice precursors, give your command and then, when she mounts, praise (or click) and reward. Or, if this seems a little bizarre for the park crowd to witness, try to get her to mount your leg or some consenting dog in another context so you have opportunities to supply your cue and reward. You need plenty of pairings to make the association (>40). Then you can start oscillating commanded/rewarded mounts with uncommanded/unrewarded ones and watch the uncommanded ones die a slow death. Plus you get a neat, if twisted, trick (my command for El Diablo to hump my leg is "darling, we're not doing that now...").

If the mounting behavior is highly resistant to a well-executed assault with these techniques and becomes more frequent and intense, the next step is to have her hormones checked out if you're still worried.

DOGS ARE FROM NEPTUNE

Geriatric Barking

A friend has a fourteen-year-old collie mix that, as of two weeks ago, has taken up the habit of standing at the front door and barking. I asked my friend if there have been any unusual outside distractions and she said that it has been quiet.

She and her husband recently moved to this new home but Katie has had at least four months to acclimate. As her walker, I've never noticed her to be at all excitable at the front door. She's usually asleep on her couch. The owner insists that this is a new behavior.

Any suggestions?

If this were low-threshold watchdog barking, I would suggest developing a "quiet" command to turn Katie off after she has had a few barks at something. However, let's first rule out whether Katie is simply getting a little dotty in her old age. Geriatric dogs often get quirky behaviors like this. It doesn't mean anything about her quality of life or health necessarily, although it would certainly be worthwhile having her looked at by her vet. If there have been any other changes in her behavior, notably anything looking like separation anxiety, restlessness, pacing or difficulty settling down overnight, these are worth mentioning at the consult.

The four months may seem like ample time to you and me for a dog to get used to a new home but it's possible that it still feels strange to Katie. It would be helpful to develop a good, solid routine to her days if there isn't one already. After the vet has worked her up, the best way to deal with the barking when it happens is to redirect her attention, snap her into another mode. Good choices are phrases with long-standing association, such as "do you want to..." (go for a walk, go get a cookie, go outside) or "where is..." (your leash, your toy, name of family member). Follow it up with action.

If there is any precursor to her barking - some identifiable trigger in the environment or a wind-up behavior, such as orienting or approaching the door - the attempt to distract her can be done pre-emptively, i.e. before she has begun barking. This will avoid the possibility of your redirection rewarding the barking. I would also look more critically at what is setting her off. Is there any pattern? What is happening immediately before she starts? What was the context surrounding the first episode? This kind of detective work often yields important insights.

If there is no compelling reason to modify it, such as complaints from the neighbors or it going on interminably, it could be simply ignored. This may weaken it, especially if it has been buying her attention from her owners. I feel, as many do, extra affection and protectiveness towards veteran dogs and am inclined to grant them some license to have idiosyncrasies. My main concern is the potential significance of such a change in behavior in an older dog vis à vis her health. This is why I would follow through with the check-up regardless of whether they wish to modify the behavior or not.

DOGS ARE FROM NEPTUNE

Dirt and Stool Eating

My family and I recently purchased a Weimaraner puppy. He is now 11 weeks old and loves to eat junk. He eats just about everything but seems to really enjoy eating dirt. He sticks his nose into flowerpots and eats the dirt inside them. I'm afraid that it may be bad for him. We tell him not to but he continues whenever he gets the chance. Is there a way we can make him stop?

Puppies are basically vehicles to transport their mouths around. So, it's understandable that your boy is eating plant dirt. It's not as bad for him as much as it is annoying for us. There are a couple of keys to nipping habits like this.

First, whenever you are unable to supervise, confine the puppy to a thoroughly dog-proofed room or pen (if he is housetrained) or to a crate (if there are any doubts whatsoever about his housetraining). This piece of advice goes for all puppies that age with or without a dirt-eating habit, by the way. Anyone who lets a puppy or untrained dog loose in their house, or even part of their house, unsupervised, is asking for it. And, when I say "supervise," I mean active eyes-on-him-every-second supervision. Some people consider supervision to mean being in the same room with the dog. The reason for such tight supervision is timing, which I'll go into in a minute.

A dog-proofed confinement area has absolutely nothing in it that the dog can destroy. No drapes, furniture, baseboard moldings, wires or personal items. Some people do not have a room that is suitable so they must opt for either a crate or an ex-pen. Ex-pens are much roomier than crates. They are folding corrals that look like playpens. These items are available from better pet supply houses and from mail order catalogues. The main thing is that there is a safe area to keep the puppy when you are not watching him.

When you are available to supervise, give him access to non-confinement areas, including where he can get at the plants. Have

106

a supply of his own toys always present and praise whenever he displays interest in them. The instant you see him sniffing at the plant, about to indulge, explode into an urgent series of "AH! AH! AH! AH!" to interrupt him. As soon as he ceases, take the pressure right off, become sweet again and say "thank you!" Then, immediately coach him over to one of his own chew toys. There are three classic errors people make when redirecting dogs:

1) Slow interruption: There is a ton, no, several tons, of difference between interrupting a dog as he is about to go in the dirt vs. correcting him after one or two, or worse, mouthfuls. If there is dirt in his mouth, it is a late interruption, which is much, much, much weaker than a well-timed one. It's almost as though some biological accountant in the dog figures "yeah, but it was worth it." Not only might he keep trying when you're around, he is also finding out how tasty and fun dirt is and might end up reserving his dirt habit for when you are gone, which greatly compounds things later on. Every poorly timed interruption sets you back in training. Remember, the whole point is to actively condition him to go for the right thing when he gets the urge, not to punish out the wrong thing and hope he then guesses right by default. To accomplish this, your intervention must come at the right instant.

People with stool eaters (not to mention diggers) are often guilty of quite abysmal timing. The dog does it in the yard, comes in and gets reprimanded many minutes after the onset of the act. Or, the dog is caught "most of the time" but not always; this is doomed to failure. If you want to end stool eating, you have to catch the dog **every time** until he is hooked on your alternative. A period of **perfect** control is necessary to end this habit. This means yard clean up must be immediate during the training period and the only time the dog is given access to stools is when he is staked out by an alert owner. It's a sting, in other words. Stings can be performed on the street, in the park or wherever the dog tries the behavior. Obviously this requires some control-freak tendencies.

DOGS ARE FROM NEPTUNE

Products like "Forbid" can be put in the dog's food to make the resulting stool unpalatable. The advantage of this is, of course, timing, not to mention removing the association of the aversive from you to the stool itself. It works on some dogs but not others. If your dog goes for the feces of other dogs as well as his own, lace a couple of different dogs' food with the product and then strategically place their stools in striking range.

2) Lack of intensity or gradual escalation of intensity: If your puppy was not going for dirt, but for rat poison, how would you react? Everyone becomes a very hot trainer when there are real stakes (for instance, if you are lucky enough to catch a budding stool eater on his first trial, most peoples' reaction is sufficiently dramatic that there is never a second try). They are fast, explosive and focused. For the routine stuff, however, many owners chant "nooooo" at the dog with very little effect other than diluting the word. Then, they gradually escalate the volume or harshness. This can culminate in a dog that will ignore impressive levels of loudness and meanness.

Remember, if you *wanted* to desensitize a dog to something like the word "no," the way to do it would be to say it a lot at a tolerable volume, never have it predict anything and then gradually increase the intensity, contingent on continued non-response. Ironically, although people struggle with this instruction when it comes to phobia habituation, where desensitization is desired, they do expert jobs at getting their dogs to ignore their "no" type commands.

The reason people fall into this trap is that they hope or presume the dog's understanding of their emotion or intention will suffice to dissuade him. This is a seriously flawed premise. So, when interrupting dogs from plants, shoes, forbidden places etc., be fast and big, right off the bat. Act as you would if it were something highly dangerous.

3) Lack of alternative. This is the most important thing. The puppy is going for plant dirt because he wants to play, explore and put stuff in his mouth. He is not "bad." He is a "dog." No

one put a gun to your head and made you buy a dog. If you don't want dog behavior, avoid dogs. Now, what **legal** activity can he engage in that will meet most or all of these requirements? What kinds of chew toys does he have? Does he use them? If not, why not? Do you stuff Kongs and bones for him as puzzles for part of his daily food ration? Is the puppy stimulated in other ways, like training and problem solving? Does he get to play fetch or tug every day? Is he getting walked regularly? Does he get to play with other dogs? If you have not addressed these questions, you have the core of your problem. You're not alone, if this is an issue, by the way. Most domestic dogs are pretty badly understimulated. Remember, the redirection stuff is icing. Provision of an adequate environment is the cake.

After you institute a regime, there will come a time when you will remark that it's been weeks since he's even tried to go for plant dirt or other forbidden things. At that point, you may gradually begin to relax your surveillance. If he doesn't prove trustworthy, tighten things up again for a while.

DOGS ARE FROM NEPTUNE

OBEDIENCE

Off Leash Control

I live in New Zealand where it is impossible to get any help training your dog unless you are prepared to use J&P ("jerk & praise," ed.), shock collars etc.

I have a four-year-old spayed Tibetan Terrier bitch named Tess.

We have done three J&P classes. At a year old, she started bolting every time she was off lead. In despair I sent her to an animal behaviorist recommended by my vet. He used a shock collar on her and I got her back a month later "shell-shocked," with the advice that she still wasn't totally "reliable" and that I would have to keep a shock collar on her permanently.

I wasn't prepared to do this so I went back to basics, running her on a long line etc. Things improved a little. Then a new behaviorist came on the scene and I gave him a try. He used extremely rough J&P, even suggesting I place the lead around a strong post to practise jerking as hard as possible!

Late last year I discovered clicker training, have gotten Gary Wilkes video, clickers, Don't Shoot The Dog, A Dog and a Dolphin and have just finished The Culture Clash.

In the meantime, Tess has twice chased sheep and has become very aggressive towards small dogs. She runs at them, hackles up, teeth bared and any form of submission from the small dog is met by a nip from Tess. I socialized her in every way I could as a puppy but I only got her as a 16 week-old. This dog aggression didn't start until she was about 2. She has been attacked by a boxer, a Rottie and a Staffy. Because of the sheep problem and the small dog problem I now have very few places I can exercise

111

DOGS ARE FROM NEPTUNE

her off lead as her recall goes to the wind if she sees a dog/sheep/picnic.

In the mornings we walk to work together along a beach. All the other dogs are off lead and she is on a flexi. I can't let her off as houses border the beach and she would just run into them searching for food. I think the frustration of watching the other dogs off lead is making things worse. If any approach her, she is very aggressive even though I do my utmost to keep a slack lead, remain calm, reward for no hackles/growling etc.

Around home, work, and on the lead her sit/down/stays are very good. She is enjoying clicker training but is difficult to motivate. She is not interested in a Frisbee; will chase a ball about three times (these days I stop after one or two throws to try and increase her interest); her tug toy only seems to be of interest to her in the evenings. I would really appreciate some help with recalls as well as the sheep and dog aggression problem I have. I'm working alone here in NZ as no one has even heard of C&T.

Here are my suggestions:

1) If Tess is in normal-to-good health, go all out food-training her. Condition the clicker to a variety of treats, including but not limited to liver, sliced hot-dogs, cheese, tiny cookies and cubed Rollover (salami-style dog food/treat). Mix it up. Then, once you've done a couple of weeks of practicing at home and in your yard - especially recalls and a "watch me" command - cut her meal ration to 50%. Also, withhold her most preferred two or three treats with one exception: off lead, in public recalls. This is where she will make up the caloric deficit.

    Practise recalls every day on the beach or in other public places. If you're nervous, start off with her dragging a long line (for insurance). When you feel more confident about her recall, have her off leash. The reward system is extremely important. The rewards must be extremely good. She should be hungry (hence the rationing - you can return to a normal regime when she is reliable). Initially, she should win the game at least half the time. This means manipulating the level of difficulty. The easiest recalls will be when she is relatively close to you and there are no distractions (dogs/sheep/picnics etc.). Distance and distraction will increase the level of difficulty.

To start off, do a few conservative, easy ones: close up, low distraction. When she is sitting right in front of you, hit the clicker and then (and only then) dig into your pouch for the food reward. When she does well and makes no mistakes, increase the difficulty. You can do this by adding distance or by calling when there is a more challenging. When she does well at this, bump up the difficulty again. If you get nothing, bump down the difficulty to something between where you had perfection and where it fell apart.

Have two or three different, highly coveted kinds of food rewards in your pouch. Do not "preview" these for her. She will find out what's in there by performing. Develop a quality control system. For example, let's say Tess' favorite reward is cheese flavored hot dogs. Her second favorite is pretzels and her third favorite is baked liver bits. A five-tier system could be:

Reward level #1: given less than 10% of the time. Consists of a random combo of the above but always includes at least two cheese dog slices and some of the other stuff. Each component of the reward is given individually (rather than as a handful), beginning and ending with the cheese dogs (e.g. cheese dog-liver-liver-pretzel-cheese dog-cheese dog).

Reward level #2: given also about 10% of the time. Consists of a cheese dog slice, occasionally a "double" for responses which don't quite make it to level #1, plus praise.

Reward level #3: given 15% of the time. Consists of a pretzel or two and praise.

Reward level #4: given 15% of the time. Consists of a liver bit or two and praise.

Reward level #5: given the other 50% of the time. Consists of "thank you very much" (praise only).

Level 1 is for unexpectedly good responses, much better than you ever would have thought she would give under the conditions. Level 2 is for excellent responses at the level you're working at. Level 3 is for very good responses. Level 4 is for good enough responses. Level 5 is for duds, where you had to "help."

If you find you're busting out of the system (either over-dispensing or under-dispensing near the top or bottom), it means it is time to adjust the standard you are demanding. You may need to increase or reduce distraction, distance, or both.

When she is unstumpable, you will put her on an intermittent reinforcement schedule. This gradual reduction in reward frequency is very important for maintaining strong responses. There is a ton of information on reinforcement schedules in your books.

2) If they are not full-fledged fights, ignore her aggressive displays at dogs. Either turn and briskly walk the other way or, if you think you have a chance, try a recall. Meeting random dogs needs to become more of a non-event. Too much of the time, owner-intervention, however well meant, heats things up rather than cooling them down. When she passes dogs peacefully or investigates without incident, heap on the praise and, as soon as the dog has passed, click and treat her.

3) Cease any coercive techniques: the J&P and shock.

4) Once your recalls are top-notch, use the beach as setting for trick training using your clicker.

5) If the sheep chasing seems compulsive (every possible opportunity, she chases), keep her on leash around sheep. This is the easiest solution, provided you don't live on a sheep farm. If sheep are omnipresent, you'll have to work specifically on that area. If her sheep chasing is occasional and seems less highly motivated, add it as a distraction on your recall exercises.

6) Do you know anyone with novel (to her), well-socialized dogs who might befriend her? If yes, get the dogs together for extended sessions in some secure area (in someone's house or fenced yard). Ignore any initial tension or fisticuffs if it is not serious. Leave them together even if they seem bored or are ignoring each other. Boredom often leads to play ("what to do...what to do...ah, a dog") which leads to development of social repertoire etc. which can only help you.

I am amazed that more sophisticated training is not available in a fabulous country like New Zealand.

DOGS ARE FROM NEPTUNE

Stay Breaking

I have a four year old neutered English Staffy service dog, Jack, trained with OC (operant conditioning, ed.) and a clicker, who works splendidly at assistance tasks. We have one major problem, and that's breaking sit and down stays when I'm giving demos and seminars, and busy talking. He does not break his stays when he knows he is being watched, ever.

I have tried setting him up for success, by getting people to interact with me, and watching his body language from my peripheral vision, and reinforcing him just BEFORE he breaks. It works as long as I'm being very watchful, but if I forget to watch him, he'll break every time.

Is there a way of approaching this problem without using aversives?

Great question!! Discrimination learning can drive trainers nuts when it works against us. We cook up more and more sophisticated set-ups and they root out finer and finer perceptible differences and continue to respond selectively only when the contingencies are in effect.

It's possible, reading your description, that when Jack breaks, it isn't just a case of the behavior "stay" crumbling at that second but that this movement is being reinforced. So, while you've been building up the strength of "stay," something in the environment has been strengthening "break," each under specific conditions. Likely candidates for reinforcers for breaking are: exploration, (sniffing, vacuuming etc.), social contact and proprioceptal/stretch (i.e. the act of movement or position change itself can be reinforcing, especially after a long period of non-movement).

Here are a few things to try:

1) Refine your set-ups even more to blur the discrimination. This means taking stabs at what key stimulus (i) the dog is using to discriminate between training and real life and setting this up

116

till you get the problem. In other words, you have to elicit the problem before you can work on it. My guess is that the key stimuli in this case are: you projecting your voice, you taking your eyes/focus totally off the dog, gesticulation as one does while teaching a group, the presence of handlers/dogs in particular configurations or numbers, and possibly the reinforcement schedule itself (i.e. we tend to reinforce less in performance situations than in training and this is highly salient).

So, to test, bump up the realism of these elements separately and in combos and see if you start getting breaks. When you have experimented and noted all the things that make the breaking come to life, you can start training, by pushing the average as you have already been doing (reinforcing before breaks) or by incorporating a no-reward signal, described in #3.

2) Blur it the other way: rather than making your training more like real life, make real life more like training. The best possible simulation is always the situation itself, in all its richness. But, this is the situation that built the problem in the first place so, by definition, is a training blind spot. The easiest way out of this corner is to use double handling. Someone else fills the role of designated stay trainer - reinforcing stays - while you teach naturally. The person should be different every time and stationed randomly so that they do not become a new discriminative stimulus. Also, the schedule, once the stay is strong, needs to be whittled down sufficiently to mask the absence of a designated.

3) Introduce a conditioned negative punisher - the opposite of a clicker. This is the signaling of the removal of ongoing or imminent reward. People think the opposite of reinforcement is punishment but the opposite of reinforcement is no reinforcement. The key element in orchestrating negative punishment in practical dog training is informing the dog that he has just made a critical error - and with clicker-like precision timing - that has cost him reinforcement. This is where the *conditioned* negative punisher comes in. It is

repeatedly paired with a pointed loss, removal or absence of reinforcement.

It is necessary that, once you signal "too bad!" or whatever your No-Reward-Mark (NRM) is, the dog not be reinforced, either by you or by the environment. This means preventing him from collecting whatever he might be after. If you signal no-reward and he proceeds to sniff around and this is reinforcing, your NRM will lose its charge. We call this "direct access," as opposed to accessing reinforcers by complying with the trainer. So, as soon as he starts to break, signal him that he has lost the game and then start another (stay) trial. You must be in a position to put your money where your mouth is, both with reward and reward removal (part of this is preventing direct access), in order to effectively animal-train. This is why it is such a control-freak friendly endeavor.

If there is, in fact, something that has been reinforcing stay breaks at times, this is an exploitable reinforcer you may sometimes wish to use. When he has made the grade with his stay, you can click and then grant him access: "go vacuum," "go see the dog," "stretch time" or whatever your detective work has identified. Most of the time, you will probably reinforce conventionally, with food.

To charge up your NRM, you must precede it with removal of or absence of expected reinforcement. To get a lot of repeated trials to demonstrate the trend, you can do some level-appropriate distraction training, pinning the NRM on boo-boos that will correlate with no reinforcement. Proof any behaviors you like, not just stays, to accomplish this. In beginner dogs, we use simple impulse control exercises to get them up to speed - set ups to hammer in the concepts "stay," "don't lunge," "don't pull" and "don't jump up." On each trial the dog is either reinforced or gets a NRM that comes to mean no reinforcement on that trial. As the behavior gets conditioned, so does the NRM (sort of like reverse clicker training on the fly). Make sure, when you do this, that you monitor the standard. If the dog is not getting reinforced often enough, he stops playing the game. Losing dogs during installation of NRM's is inefficient time management.

Note that this is not the same as a conditioned stimulus for operant variability (the "try something else" signal). A NRM means simply "you just blew it!" and its function is to *decrease* the frequency of the behavior preceding it, which is why it is classified as a punisher.

DOGS ARE FROM NEPTUNE

Heeling on Street

I have a 22-month old Golden who has been going to leash-correction style training classes for a year. I am not confident the training he went through was beneficial.

Heeling - Raiden doesn't pull on the leash but he is always trying to stay just a couple of inches ahead of my feet. I have tried stopping dead in my tracks every time he begins to pass my feet; he stops and backs up.

Also, I take Raiden out to the park and attach him to a 50 feet rope for exercise. I let him sniff around but usually find myself having to jerk on the rope and tell him "let's go" to get him to move on. Any suggestions?

Good going fixing pulling in your Golden.

Heeling is a tough command for dogs. It's not only a precise position with a moving target and bonus features like "sit when I stop" and, possibly, "maintain eye contact," it's expected for extended durations and often around high ambient distraction. It's not surprising that achieving perfection is elusive and, when it is achieved, it's for competition exercises that last for a minute or two at the most.

The standard of heeling we teach dogs in formal obedience classes is not, in my opinion, the standard we should expect from our dogs for long durations while out on a walk. Heel him across streets or past certain features you want him to not investigate. Heel him to practise for the ring. But, the rest of the time, I would be inclined to settle for more of a compromise, another non-heeling gear for use on walks.

For this on-a-walk gear, Raiden will make the following concessions: "I will stay more or less on one side of you, behave in a civilized way towards people and dogs, never tighten the leash, and heel for those specific stretches where it is asked." Your concessions: "You may sniff all you want unless you're told to heel, and when heeling is demanded it will be kept brief and good performances will be rewarded. You may meet dogs and investigate things of interest to you as long as you don't tighten the leash." A regime such as this will protect your heeling.

To clean up the forged heel position, you can

1) carry on with your current system, perhaps with a NRM - No Reward Mark - to sharpen up your timing: when he crosses the line and starts to forge, instantly tell him "ooh! too bad!" and then back up and re-do the stretch till he gets it right - forward progress is contingent on correct position,

2) try prompting the position you want and then fading the prompt or

3) try pure shaping.

The usual prompt is a toy or bait target placed strategically on the side rather than front of your body and then faded upwards. Pant seams are perfect for this. Front or face target placement sometimes elicits a too-forged or wrapped position. Pocket squeakies can be put right in your armpit. If you have been using a formal attention command, switching the target from your face to the outside of your shoulder or upper arm will sometimes buy you a couple of inches back with a bigger dog without any other training intervention.

Probably the best thing to do is to hammer away at perfecting your position in low distraction (i.e. not while on a walk) using shaping. Select the best short (several second) stretches for reward. Part of the reason I like this option is that it develops the most skill in the trainer.   There is no substitute for a good eye for a rewardable response. If you haven't done a lot of shaping, the hardest part is the early stage where "you have to reward *something*" and that something is, by definition, a sample of what the dog is already doing. Accept that you can't have the final product that is pictured in your head, yet. You have to reward the best the dog is *already* offering. This takes discipline. If the dog is green at being shaped, reward about half the trials. This means a series of short bursts of heeling, half of which you reward, not because they're brilliant but because they're slightly less pathetic than the ones you're not rewarding.

When you discover that the average has gone up, you can raise your standard till you're rewarding about half the time again. And so on. Crank it up as high as you'd like in this fashion. The standard will have to do with the dog restraining himself from forging. A lot of people prompt the position with a tap stick and then. This is a bit aversive and you won't be forced to develop your eye for shaping.

I'm not wild about the rope jerk to get the dog to move on. You may successfully wean off the rope but you may also get zero transference to off-lead. Try moving on when he's off leash and, if you're in a safe enough area, "losing" the dog (i.e. hiding so he has a brief "gasp! where'd he go!" panic attack and subsequently keeps closer tabs on you) to develop emotional "bungee." Or simply reward him (praise, tug, treat or fetch, whichever works) when he makes a better effort at keeping up. Again, I'd reward around half the efforts at first and ignore the others. You'll have to be disciplined enough to banish any potential "he KNOWS, why should I have to reward blah blah blah" thoughts. There's another choice, too. If he doesn't run off and comes when called on these walks, you can just let him go at his own pace.

You have the control-freak attributes of a great animal trainer. Maybe lighten up a bit.

Compulsive Greeting

My friend's Rottie used to be shy around people but she went nuts socializing him. Now he loves people. Maybe too much. If they're on a walk in the woods and he spots someone at a distance, he runs, wiggling, to greet them. He jumps up at them, sometimes on them. He's usually very responsive to his owner, and if she can get his attention before he takes off toward the people she can call him to her. But once he's on his way, nothing stops him. She doesn't want to do anything negative for fear he will associate it with people, and he had that tendency to be shy with people before. She would rather not always have to keep him on leash, because he needs off-leash exercise. Any ideas?

Kudos to your friend for her successful socialization effort. Good move to not add aversives to the mix, too. The last thing you want is a higher likelihood of rotten things happening to him when there are strangers around.

It's good that she can interrupt his charge if she catches him early enough in the sequence. I hope she's rewarding (praise good, treat or tug better) his snappy returns. If so, she's already on the right track. To beef up the effort, there are a few things she can do:

1) increase the level of difficulty of his returns, especially how late in the sequence she can get a successful recall, and/or

2) condition an automatic sit-to-greet people till it outweighs jumping and/or

3) condition an automatic return-to-owner when he eyeballs people

Which of the above she does depends on how many lines of defense she wants and, obviously, on the amount of time she wants to spend training.

Interrupting charging dogs with recalls is an interesting training challenge. It's not surprising that "once he's on his way, nothing

123

stops him." Behaviors like prey chasing (squirrels, bicycles etc.) and greeting (like this Rottie) have a compulsive flavor to them. Dogs can learn to snap out of them but it takes a fair amount of rehearsal. The key to achieving progress is multiple trials: sessions outside where she practises calling him off in mid-charge over and over from the same person, potently rewarding nice responses.

There is virtually no chance of a rewardable response on the first couple of passes but re-enacting the same approach to the same person will start to produce the "Oh, you again" reaction in the dog. His excitement will diminish and, at some point, he will attend to the command. Reward time. Do a few more for consolidation and quit the session or else change people to get the excitement back up again. Then repeat to the point of the "oh, you again"/rewardable response (my favorite way is to do three or four people in succession to the "OYA" point in each session). In subsequent training sessions, the number of trials it takes for the rewardable response to kick in will diminish. One day, it will kick in on the first trial, which is what she's after. Yippee.

It's important that his wrong responses - the jumps - don't get reinforced and this part can be hard to engineer. The person the dog is greeting should absolutely ignore the dog, like a statue. For some dogs, this is sufficient but, for others, merely completing the approach/jump sequence is self-reinforcing. If you're a compulsive clean freak, think of how you feel before you clean the house, and after. There's no doubt that just **completing** the behavior you feel pressure to perform is reinforcing. It's not a perfect analogy but it gives us some empathy for dogs who "insist" on "disobeying" obedience commands when their "must greet/appease" buttons get pushed. (Interestingly, traditional dog training would dictate the use of aversives here, which would be ill advised.)

If your friend does not make significant progress by having the person ignore the dog, she will need to come up with a way to mechanically prevent completion of the sequence (such as the person disappearing or a barrier). This is no easy feat and the whole issue is further compounded by a possible initial increase in motivation to greet created by the deprivation at a key moment. Happily, most dogs come along nicely with the repeated trials.

She can also practise recalls from contrary motion out of context during fetch games or away from pre-set toy or food "magnets." This will often get a foot in the door on the more recalcitrant cases. We want this dog ceasing motion, whirling around and completing recalls in his sleep.

Conditioning an automatic sit-to-greet is a similar process. It requires rehearsal sessions with people who know what to do: be cold and withholding when he jumps, be able to effectively command or lure the first half dozen sits and then be warm and fuzzy and/or give (hidden) food rewards when he complies. The dog must only meet people who are in on it until he is performing error-free for intermittent rewards before he is unleashed (pardon the pun) on the real world. Otherwise he may learn to discriminate your set-ups from life. We hate this.

The "automatic recall" is a third line of defense. If your friend is alert and calls him as soon as he orients toward any person he sees on the street, her dog may become classically conditioned to run to her when he sees a person on the street (dog-sees-person predicts recall command, dog seeing person becomes conditioned stimulus). Once again, you could speed up the process with troubleshooting sessions.

Although the auto-recall doesn't address what to do when he has already misfired, it does reduce the number of misfires: "Whenever you see a person, the next thing is always a recall command; people you meet on walks are the occasion for running back to your owner." When the dog starts anticipating the command, the command can then be faded. When conditioning is done, your friend can be asleep at the switch while on walks and still get the recall when she needs it.

DOGS ARE FROM NEPTUNE

Recall off Predatory Distraction

I have a five year-old spayed female German Shorthaired Pointer and Cattle Dog mix. She was an excitable pup, but playful. We went to a traditional school that used harsh methods, and she got very wild, particularly out in the park. She'd go crazy with excitement and aggression when she saw another dog. She would run long distances and not come when called.

We went to a different school, using leadership and motivational (reward) training. She is now sociable with dogs and can be let off the lead. The one remaining problem is that she is very predatory. She needs a lot of exercise, and where I walk her, there are rabbits and ducks. She actually caught and killed a duck, and has nearly succeeded with a rabbit. We have worked on distraction training, attentiveness, recalls and building her motivation.

She is not very interested in food or toys (or in me), but we have increased her interest compared to what it was. She is now generally placid and well behaved unless she spots a bird or a rabbit. How can I use motivation to deal with this problem?

Predation is a very tough nut to crack. Sometimes it is evident early on that a dog is turned on by movement, animals etc. above and beyond normal puppy stuff. Also, with certain breeds and lines of dogs, we have the luxury of knowing some of the genetic make-up and can therefore start our prevention campaign early. The most important element in the campaign is getting the dog hooked on a target we can live with, before the dog makes its own random selection. For instance, the first line of defense against dogs chasing cars is getting them "imprinted" onto livestock (if it's a working dog), balls or Frisbees. Once they're hooked, other things will often be ignored or trampled on the way to their drug of choice.

What has happened is your girl has gotten hooked on rabbits and ducks. I understand your training hurdle: you want to train with positive reinforcement but you have nothing to offer as a reinforcer

126

that can compete with the potency of those chases. Whatever else you do, try to get her hooked on some other target, though this is unlikely on its own to reduce her interest in animals. Usually you will end up with an extra target: teach Frisbee to a flyball dog and they still like flyball boxes. They now also like Frisbees. Sometimes, however, if you find something really seductive and offer it relentlessly in the context that used to predict the former target, effectively block the former target and redirect to the new target, you can switch them over. With your dog's history, I'd venture that this is a long shot (try vigorous fetch and tug with furry stuffed animals).

There are therefore two ways to go:

1) Obtain sufficient control of the environment so that, although she will still be keen on birds and rabbits, you will dictate **when** she gets to chase. This is using Premack's Principle to exploit the distraction as a reinforcer and might qualify by your criteria as training motivationally.

2) Crack and use a heavy aversive like a shock collar to pound in a more solid recall around this particular distraction.

Here are the nuts and bolts and pluses and minuses of each strategy.

Premack's Principle states that opportunity to engage in a high probability behavior can function as a reinforcer for a lower probability behavior. It's the "eat your broccoli and then we'll discuss dessert" thing. If eating dessert is a high probability behavior and eating broccoli is not, dessert can be used as reinforcer to raise the likelihood of broccoli. Dessert is no longer a distraction, it is the reinforcer, contingent on broccoli eating. This works perfectly if you have control over the subject's access. If the subject can directly access dessert, broccoli is ignored. It can also work the other way. If, on any given day, you crave greens, we can make you eat cake in order to get your greens. In this case it would be cake first, broccoli after. The high probability behavior bar is always opened up *after* the subject coughs up the low probability behavior you want to reinforce.

This works perfectly in the laboratory, where the experimenter has terrific control of the animal's environment. The problem with the real world is controlling access to reinforcers. If they can directly access them, you can't manipulate any other behaviors. Whatever they did to directly access the reinforcer gets strengthened instead (chasing, running away, disobedience, all the stuff we hate). In the case of your dog, we want to use hunting opportunities to reinforce recalls in the presence of rabbits and ducks. Tricky.

The first obstacle may be a prohibitive one: do we ever want to grant the top reinforcer in the hierarchy, hunting? If not, we're left trying to train behaviors which conflict with hunting using reinforcers that cannot compete with hunting. We're cooked. (This may not indeed be your decision to make. There may be laws or social pressure that pre-empt ever going this route, in which case our discussion is moot.)

If you are allowed and prepared to give the dog chasing sprees (with the inevitable risk of kills) in order to train up lower probability behaviors, like recalls and walking past bunnies without becoming unglued, the next obstacle is logistics. How do we get the job done? You must be able to block access to animals until you obtain whatever the current standard of response is. Then you grant a chase: "okay! go get 'em!" Leashes and crushing verbal corrections can be used to this end but are not without complications.

Leashes can mechanically block access but are potent discriminative stimuli, i.e. noticeable to the dog, so one often ends up with response on-leash and not much response off-leash. Verbal corrections work on some dogs (Border Collies, for example, though intensely predatory have also been selectively bred with soft enough temperaments that they usually can be made to wilt mid-herd at considerable distance by a gruff shepherd's voice). Also, there's no doubt that this introduces an aversive to the process. Which brings us to the question of shock collars.

Whether or not to use aversives is always an agonizing decision. For those who strive to train using all-positives, it's a corner we hate feeling painted into. Everyone, in order to maintain psychological well being, needs to behave congruently with their values. Some train all positives and obtain the results they are after. Some may only feel comfortable training all positives regardless of the result. Some may crack and use aversives in order to get a particular result if they feel trapped. What qualifies as a worthwhile result is another question. Some only crack if the behavior in question is, in their estimation, a life-saver or quality of life-saver for the dog. Some crack for other reasons. Some may opt for aversives even if they are aware of an all-positive alternative, for reasons of perceived expediency, reliability or because it is how they are most comfortable training. Some opt to use aversives in light of all-positive alternatives for what others might view as trivial training tasks. There is a pretty broad spectrum of viewpoints, as you probably know. No one can tell you which camp you are in.

The other issue raised by aversives is technical. Because aversives carry side effects, are potentially ruinous, and are always upsetting and invasive, execution must be flawless. In the case of remote-training a recall, the trainer must have excellent timing, a cool head, a perfect understanding of the application of negative reinforcement and the willingness to pre-condition the recall properly with the collar. If these conditions are met, it is possible to get a relatively "clean" result, i.e. dog understands exactly how to avoid the shock with minimal applications thereof. It is critical, by the way, that the collar be used to train *in* a recall using negative reinforcement and not used to train *out* chasing using punishment. This distinction is very, very important.

So, you must decide where you stand on the issue of aversives in training. You must decide whether this particular problem meets the criteria for use of aversives in your value system. If it were my own dog who was a five year old hunter with successes under her belt, I would opt for a lot of management (alternative exercise and socialization strategies, leash in this park etc.) while slowly chipping away at redirecting her as well as selectively providing chases (à la Premack) when a catch and kill seem unlikely, contingent on impulse control beforehand. I might see if she's responsive to verbal corrections which would open up more training doors but I would not opt to use shock, even if I struck out without it.

Because I am personally not comfortable with shock, however, it does not mean I consider it "wrong." Recalls often encompass safety and quality of life issues and so, in my value system, lie in the gray area vis à vis use of aversives. I could definitely stretch and cook up a hypothetical case in which I might crack and advise a shock collar to install a recall. I don't blame trainers for cracking when they feel their backs are to the wall and they must achieve a result to save a dog.

The important thing is that you train in a way that allows you to live with yourself. Also, if you choose, for whatever reason, to use heavy aversives, be sure to find someone who has the requisite skill to work a remote trainer.

Pulling on Leash

I have been trying (and trying) to get our almost two year-old Dalmatian, Fraser, to walk on a loose lead. I have "made like a tree" when he pulls and we've gotten to the point where he pulls, goes nowhere, turns and creates slack in the lead. But now I'm afraid I've trained him to pull/go slack ad nauseam. He also can spend quite a long time stretched at the end of the lead air sniffing, and deaf to everything else. Help!

Red-light/green-light is a technique that works perfectly in theory: the dog learns that he moves forward only on a slack leash and so works to avoid pulling. A trainer with good timing can make the initiation of tension on the leash feel to the dog like he has just applied the "brakes." The problem with the technique, in my opinion, is that it is too patience and skill intensive, and virtually unworkable with certain dogs. For example, I would speculate that the sniffing your dog enjoys on the end of the leash dilutes to a large extent the negative consequence of you halting.

Sometimes, with anti-pull exercises, even if headway is made, the walks are still unpleasant from the residual pulling or on-off pulling you describe. An improvement which, on paper, would graph out as a dramatic decrease percentage-wise in intensity and frequency of pulling might still, in real life, make for a miserable walk. With the bigger dogs, we want, for instance, no hard lunges whatsoever.

That said, making like a tree is a great first-line technique to try. It works like a dream with some dog and handler teams, especially young puppies. If you feel, after diligent effort for a couple of weeks, that you are striking out, it's time to try other things. Your dog is not the ideal candidate for this exercise, age-wise so it's not surprising you've gotten only a partial result.

Here are more options:

1) Other anti-pulling exercises. One kind is the cause and effect type exercise, along the lines of what you've tried but perhaps with beefier consequences like distance penalties for pulling,

no-reward-marks for initiation of pulling to refine timing and food or tug rewards to reinforce stretches of loose leash walking. Another exercise involves prompting the dog back into position whenever he deviates rather than simply providing consequences as the first kind does. A third method employs aversives, either along with positive consequences and/or prompts or simply aversives by themselves.

There are dozens of variations of each of these themes, almost as many as there are trainers! You could try beefing up consequences for a couple of weeks to see what kind of headway you make. You could also try marking the initiation of pulling with "oh! too bad!" and then applying the distance penalty. And, you could prompt, for instance coaching the dog back into position whenever he starts forging ahead.

If you are on the Internet, you can get a good handle on the nuts-and-bolts of these variations by subscribing to the "Pettable" list: e-mail **majordomo@esosoft.com** and subscribe PETTABLE, where trainers troubleshoot behavior problems. You will be dazzled by the varied suggestions for anti-pulling exercises, both with and without prompts and aversives.

2) Use a halter. These are the closest things to miracle products as I've seen in the dog-biz. Amazingly, they are not that widespread in spite of their ability to dramatically and humanely cut pulling instantly in virtually every dog that wears one. Halters have been employed on other species of animals for many generations so there is a nice history of safe and effective use. Continuing public reluctance about halters may have to do with a few different factors:

•The adjustment period. Many dogs act up the first few times they wear a halter, pawing at it, rubbing their heads along the ground, balking relentlessly. It's tough on the dog and can be distressing to watch. If the owner gives in and removes it, the dog learns that the act-up behaviors work and will offer them even more vigorously next time. So, if you decide to put a halter on, do not remove it until you have a decent lull in the action. I would also suggest having it fitted by someone with halter experience, to show you how to minimize this behavior and to ensure the proper fit. After a while, even the most initially recalcitrant dogs like having their halters put on because they know it means "walk."

•The resemblance to muzzles. As soon as people see anything on the head of a dog, they assume it must be a muzzle. Halter proponents must feel like broken records, continually pointing out that it's-a-halter-it's-not-a-muzzle. Dogs can eat, drink, pant, carry things and bite when wearing a halter, although many models allow for temporary closing of the dog's mouth if the handler applies pressure in a certain way. Once the public education is up to speed, I predict we will see an explosion of halters on dogs.

•No transference. The performance on-halter does not, even with fairly extended use, transfer to off-halter walking. A halter is too potent a discriminative stimulus and pulling is too easily trained back in to allow for much generalization, unfortunately. What people **do** find, however, is that, as the dog mellows out with age and experience, the halter can be reserved for the more challenging walking situations and the dog can be easily walked on a regular collar at other times, using red-light-green-light or other standard anti-pull techniques.

Using a halter for leash-pull management does not mean you are switching over to a halter-oriented method of training, necessarily. I realize there are all kinds of exercises for teaching obedience and resolving behavior problems using halters. You can also use them strictly to make walks easier and then continue to train exactly how you have already been training. It's up to you.

I have to ask: is Fraser getting regular exercise and outlets for his hunting instincts? This is not the solution to leash-pulling but will make him a quicker study for anything involving impulse control that you try to teach him. I sometimes see young dogs in obedience classes that are so pent up from underexercise and understimulation that their curves are pretty seriously compromised, especially for the impulse control stuff, like "don't pull towards that squirrel/dog/person/leaf."

Hang in there. If you decide to train (rather than going the halter route) and one technique doesn't work, there are a myriad of others to try for this problem. It really is just a question of finding the one that does the trick on your dog.

Ringwise

I have an eight and a half year-old Old English Sheepdog who has been training in Utility for almost three years. She is not stable in the signal and go out exercises but I feel solid on the glove and articles. She has been to five or six fun matches. I entered her in a trial just for exposure and - wow! - She could not even do the glove exercise and the articles. She just stood in the pile of articles, and did not pick up the glove but just stood and looked at me.

At fun matches she can do both although she slows up on the articles. Are there any special exercises that I can do to combat stress in this dog? Her disposition is normally shy and retiring but I fail to understand how she can deteriorate so much upon presentation of the REAL ring situation. I am looking for exercises for her and exercises for me to combat this stress in the ring.

Obedience trials hold particular and interesting training challenges. Although most of the basics of the exercises are relatively straightforward to train and the tasks are given in advance (not to mention presented in static order!), there are a few things which are fiendishly difficult about obedience. Reliability is a must, i.e. performance on first command with zero tolerance of anticipation. The details and precision necessary for high scores in the sport make for some long-winded and dullish training, not for the faint of heart. Dogs can learn the fine discriminations between straight and slightly crooked, between being in or slightly out of heel position etc. but getting there is time-intensive. This part of obedience, shaving off the points to get a high score, boils down to trainer discipline and motivation: how badly does one want it?

Perhaps the most difficult thing about obedience is what's been making your obedience life miserable lately: the non-contingent nature of the performance/evaluation situation, obedience trials. If they get it right, all is well, no damage to the training job. If they get it wrong, there is an instant learning opportunity: handler standing like a post, zero consequence, zero prompting or coaching, zero re-do. Performance sometimes deteriorates on the spot or through the course of several trials in a row. This is why you sometimes see dogs whose heeling patterns begin with slow sits and end with no sits or perhaps no dog. And the trainer is often too focused on the damage to the scores to notice the damage to the training.

When the dog learns to tell this situation apart from the ones where there *are* contingencies, a ring-wise dog is born. Even without errors, trials may feel different to the dog if the schedule of reinforcement imposed by the length of routine is thinner than the dog is used to in training. Trainers must face the fact that they may end up with discrimination based on this cue, too. Bottom line: behavior is under control of its consequences and there are no consequences in the ring at licensed trials. If they stumble onto this fact, you're in trouble.

Dogs are master discriminators. They can tell your car coming up the street from any other, an arrival home which means a normal greeting vs. one which means a late punishment for a prior chewing or housetraining transgression, movement in the kitchen which means nail clippers vs. movement in the kitchen which means cookies. I had a case of a dog that was aggressive towards 8 to 9 year old boys. Fine with younger, fine with older, fine with girls. If there is anything at all to go on and it is worth their while to do so, dogs will discriminate differences in their environment and learn the contingencies associated with them. We prep dogs for obedience trials with classes, practice and matches. This will work if a) the trial simulation is good enough and b) the dog is not entered in trials prematurely.

Dogs may tell matches from trials by elements like the degree of tension in the handler, the presence or absence of environmental features like flowers on the table, corsages on the judge, the overall ambiance and, of course, the biggie: what happens in the ring when there are right and wrong responses. This is why it's dangerous to enter a trial with a dog who is not well polished or who needs reinforcement mid-routine. Untouched mistakes, both minor and major, and/or the absence of reinforcement advertise that the situation is different from training. Then, if there is anything for the dog to go on to tell this apart from training situations, you're cooked (dog: "Oh, I see! When mummy smells like adrenaline and there are lots of dogs on grooming tables, it's that no-consequence thing where I do whatever. Got it!") Once this happens, even if you fix your training problems *in training situations,* they may come to life again in the specific context of the next trial. It's important to understand that there is no malice or intent on the part of the dog. He is an innocent subject of learning laws, as we all are.

Our goal is to never let them find out that a trial is any different from a match. The way to achieve this is to *train at matches until he's perfect.* Don't go there to try and place - go there to train in the ring. Do this until you cannot stump the dog; you've fixed everything and now you're simply running through the routine. Your performances should be feedback free till the very end. Now enter a trial. There are matches and match judges who forbid training in the ring. Either ignore this and do your own thing or else avoid them altogether. It's suicide when lack of feedback underscores the difference between training and performance contexts.

You have the extra-added bonus feature of a sensitive dog that, by the sounds of her, is not confident about some of the exercises and is definitely not wild about match and trial ambiance. One thing you can do is hang out at matches or other heavy-traffic areas (like train stations and shopping malls) and put very little pressure on her at first. Just go there and let her habituate to the sights and sounds. Do this even if she has a lifetime of dog shows and trials under her belt. I think it's important for you to break the association between these places and high pressure. When, after several times going there and just having low-pressure fun, she seems okay, start doing some really easy obedience with her. If she freezes up, however slightly, there may be a different problem: she doesn't like obedience. At that point you would have to explore why. If she's happy doing simple obedience, take her on the road and repeat the procedure at another new place. Then up the obedience.

DOGS ARE FROM NEPTUNE

At other times, you can continue to work on your problem exercises. This way you are working on the two ingredients, the obedience training and the environmentally induced stress, separately. When her confidence is built up about going to busy places and you have perfected the exercises in low-stress environments, combine these two endeavors by entering matches to train in the ring. Don't go near a trial until she is flawless and stress-free in matches, however long this takes. If you want trial exposure, enter her, scratch when you get her onto the grounds and do some hanging out, training on the sidelines, cheese sandwiches etc. Take her home with data that will start to change her mind about trials being torture.

To help reduce stress in the problem exercises, you can chain your signals and first go-out together, which may help the go-out targeting as well as creating some "flow" (motivation to drive towards the end of the routine). Because they are always presented in order and the go-out location tends to be the location where the dog just completed the signals, exploit this and pattern-train it (sorry "thinking dog" people...). This gives a bit of mental map to an exercise that can be tricky for the dog due to its multiple targets: sometimes it's baby-gates, sometimes curtains, sometimes a wall etc. So, you train the dog to "run back to the place where you just did the signals."

For a stress-prone dog, "do position changes far away in a new environment" and "run away from me in a new environment" can be anxiety provoking. Is she comfortable doing exercises involving distance in general? If not, this is another specific element you can tackle. There is a lot of work away from the handler in utility and this magnifies anxiety-related problems. I also find that many trainers over-estimate their dogs' understanding of a three-way position change discrimination and presume learning after witnessing some correct performances. You can never go wrong doing tons of games which test whether she really, really, really "gets" stand vs. down vs. sit. Plus, making it into a game may inject some fun into what has gotten serious for her. I would approach obedience as I would teaching her cute tricks.

138

If you're getting stressed out in the ring, there are a number of helpful techniques. One of the best is visualization, mentally taking yourself through a trial while in a relaxed state. The more detailed and vivid - complete with looks on handlers' faces, the sweat-marks of the dogs' pads on the mat, the smell of the judges' cologne, the steward calling your number - the better. Then, go into your mental ring, look warmly at your dog and throw it away: have a good time, do the tricks and, afterwards, a big reward for your dog regardless of performance. Now, of course, your performance can and should be perfect in your visualization! Do this, with lots of variations in the details, until it feels old hat. When the real trial day finally comes, again, throw it away by investing zero stake in the outcome.

DOGS ARE FROM NEPTUNE

FEAR & ANXIETY

Traffic Anxiety

Avery, my two and a half year-old yellow Labrador has been going to the park almost every day for the past two years. There, he plays with other dogs and runs like mad to retrieve tennis balls. During his hour in the park, he usually has one normal bowel movement.

When we go for walks on city sidewalks, he behaves well and eliminates normally but then invariably produces some diarrhea a bit later into the walk. When we go jogging on the mountain, he drags far behind at the end of the leash or just stops dead so that I must coax him with treats to get him to walk by my side. Even after he has relieved himself, including the diarrhea, he drags. The run down is usually not a problem but dragging him up to the summit is not fun. I have tried to praise and reward him when he walks beside me but he is not catching on, and the beginning of every walk is a battle. This went on all through last summer, too.

Could he hate one of the loveliest spots in the city so much? Could walking with me be so traumatic? How can I get my dog to get as much pleasure from running on the mountain as I? Leaving him at home seems a shame.

P.S. He may have some orthopedic issues from his past - he was injured when hit by a car as a puppy

I empathize with your puzzlement: here is Avery who runs like a maniac in the park yet won't jog with you (forget about scenery providing any reinforcement, by the way: "loveliness" is lost on dogs).

DOGS ARE FROM NEPTUNE

There are a couple of things to knock around here:

1) potential physical limitations and

2) learning effects

Both may be at play to differing degrees. The first thing to appreciate is general vs. task-specific exercise tolerance. We don't know if Avery's regular running and rough&tumble with dogs in the park give him the conditioning necessary for long-duration roadwork or for hills. Although it seems to be the beginning of the jog he balks most at, this simply might mean he has learned to get poky to reduce or defer a task that has proven to be uncomfortable in the past.

It is well understood from human sports medicine that fitness for bicycling does not confer perfect running ability, nor does weight training prep you for tennis. Cross training has benefits that can give you an edge in your first sport but it doesn't give you the basic muscle/endurance specs of that first sport if these are missing. It's adjunctive. It could be, for instance, that Avery's park activities are very stop-start (anaerobic) which doesn't adequately prepare him for the cardio-intensive jog. The surface may also be a factor. If he's used to running on grass, concrete or gravel may be very tough on his feet and joints. This combined with his orthopedic history makes me want to get him thoroughly evaluated for this activity by a vet with some sports/orthopedic experience.

Bottom line: we are over our heads here. We don't know if there is a physical factor(s). Let's do our best to find out. It may simply be that you have to gradually build up his stamina.

The next possibility concerns stress. The biggest clue for this is the diarrhea, which never happens in the dog park but happens regularly on roadwork and street walks. The first hypothesis that springs to mind is anxiety association with traffic. If he had a rough scare from a car accident, streets, sidewalks, the sound and/or sight of cars may be giving him some anxiety that is not easy to read. It could explain both the diarrhea and the pokiness. And, there may be another association at work. If on-leash walking or jogging is linked to traffic, on-leash jogging on the mountain may "feel" the same way.

In other words, in your mind, the jog on the mountain is like a run in the park as it has the elements of nature and running but in Avery's mind, the jog on the mountain is like traffic-proximal walks or jogs as it has the elements of leash, surface and jogging. Again, we don't know but it's worth looking into. You can attack this in two ways: by addressing the original anxiety about traffic, if it exists, and by changing the jogging-on-mountain "picture" so that it feels more to him like the in-park runs he already enjoys.

For instance, if it's safe and logistically feasible (for example, by going at a non-crowded time of day), try mountain-jogs with him off-leash. Also, is there any way to maximize him being on a vegetation-covered surface if this is part of the issue? This would be helpful until he has learned to discriminate the mountain-jog surface from the street (at the moment, your cajoling and frustration may be further linking the two!)

It may be that Avery simply would prefer a slower pace or not going to the summit and has learned that pokiness works, to a certain extent. You may also have been inadvertently rewarding pokiness with your well-meant lures and encouragement. One of the most common traps in dog training is the confusing of an antecedent (command, prompt, lure) with a consequence (reward, punishment) of behavior. Maybe you have been trying to prompt or lure a faster pace with cookies and encouragement and Avery has learned that pokiness produces the consequence of cookies and encouragement.

Part of the issue lies in the timing of initiation. For most dogs, a conditioned reinforcer they often hang their hats on is the appearance on the scene of the primary reinforcer, because it is the supreme reliable predictor: the sight of the cookie predicts cookie, even better than pocket-reaching or other events. So, we need to recognize that hauling out a cookie to prompt a faster pace may make him move a little faster before he gains the actual cookie (and thus, by the book, reward "faster pace") but that its as lure is a conditioned reinforcer for what was going on at that moment: pokiness. (Avery: "Okay, if I slow down, she reaches for the cookies, we play the jog game briefly and I get one. To get another round of the game, I simply slow down. Neat.") One of the beautiful things about clicker training is how it focuses the trainer on the timing of the conditioned reinforcer by formalizing the process. The actual delivery of the primary is parenthetical.

The solution is to selectively reward *best approximations of pace* with the pouch-opening, appearance of cookies and baby-talk instead of using these as lures and assuming the only reinforcing event is the actual delivery of cookies. Accept some of what he's already giving you and ignore the rest (including stopping dead). Recognize that admonitions, encouragement, luring and guilt-trips are all probably reinforcers of the pace he's at when you initiate them. This means doing some walks with training in mind rather than exercise but, in the long run, it's worth it. Pace is a nice, clear-cut, measurable criterion to shape for, luckily. Your current jog is a bit "sink or swim," criteria-wise.

Another idea is to have a goal for him at the summit. You may have to abandon the hope that he will find jogging inherently fun as you do. He may and he may not when you have sorted out the athletic and training issues (hey, I hate the Stairmaster, but it gives me a License to Eat). But, even if he doesn't, make the jog the means to an end: some fabulous event for him at the top of the jog: ice cream, ball game, hug-a-thon, you know what would turn him on the most. Once you have something, supply it religiously at the top regardless of his performance on the way (which, of course, you will work on).

Happy jogging.

Mild Separation Anxiety

Maude is a ten-year old wheaten terrier in good health.

Last weekend we left her with a house sitter. Diet needs, walks, etc. were all taken care of. BUT Maude left presents in between visits, something she has never done. The sitter came more often, but Maude still left messes. We returned home, and Maude has left presents on carpeted areas three of the last five days despite regular walks. She seems upset when we leave and yet has never had a problem being alone before this.

The vet thinks her behavior has to do with separation anxiety. I just don't know what to do to reverse the course.

We have a crate, which she is not happy about after all these years of freedom. I have used vinegar, fancy deodorants, and have taken to leaving food treats where she defecated on the principle that dogs don't soil where they eat or drink. All to no avail.

I must teach my darling old dog some new tricks.

It's possible that Maude's first couple of accidents were stress-related but that subsequent transgressions mean simply that she has learned new rules. When dogs get sick or very upset they may eliminate indoors. Usually it's a one-shot deal and normal habits kick back in subsequently. But, if it happens more than once, especially if the mistakes are not caught, there's a risk of the dog learning a new rule: it is, in fact, safe to eliminate indoors!!! They accidentally stumbled onto proof of this. It's as though the dog thinks "How interesting! And here was I holding it in all these years!!" So, rule this out first by going back to basics for a week or two: treat her as though she knows nothing. Supervise or crate when she is indoors and not recently emptied, reward all instances of outdoor elimination etc.

After ruling this and health issues out, I agree with your vet that the next thing to rule out is separation anxiety. After ten years of perfection, if a healthy dog breaks training, the first question to ask is "any changes in her life or routine?" In this case, the likelihood is that the weekend away kicked off the angst about being alone and this sensitized her to your subsequent departures, even though these were of normal, or even abbreviated, length. A little detective work can firm up the diagnosis:

1) Does she seem anxious when you are getting ready to leave her alone? The tip-offs are restlessness, salivation, pacing, shadowing you around etc.

2) Is there a prolonged "relief" type greeting when you come home? Most dogs greet their owners excitedly after absences but dogs with separation anxiety are even more intense. Often their greeting doesn't subside and they are still excited minutes later.

3) Does Maude have any history of vocalizing or destructiveness when alone? Is she a clingy type?

4) Are the accidents only occurring in your absence or is she sneaking any in behind your back when you are home? If she is also making mistakes when you are at home, this would point towards a health problem or housetraining regression, not separation anxiety.

If it is separation anxiety, normal housetraining measures are not the answer. This is an emotional problem. Separation anxiety responds extremely well to desensitization. The key thing is that the dog experience being left alone without feeling anxious. To accomplish this, the duration of the absence is shaved way down. Depending on the severity of the anxiety, a program may start with many trials involving the pre-departure ritual (keys, shoes etc.) only, or with brief (1-10 second) absences right off the bat. In either case, progress is built only on success: the dog must be completely without anxiety at whatever level you are on before increasing the length of the absence.

Treating separation anxiety is labor-intensive for the owner who must tolerate quite slow progress in the early stages. You can literally spend several training sessions getting the dog relaxed about reaching for your briefcase. It is also necessary to temporarily suspend "real life" absences that could undermine the program: these are, by definition, above her current level in the exercises. There is a potential way around this with a safety cue, some key difference between the exercise "picture" and real life "picture" which informs the dog whether it is about to be a tolerable or anxiety-producing length of absence and thus protects the program. However, progress is usually optimal if absences are suspended while the dog is in training.

If her case is as mild as it sounds, you may be able to resolve it much more quickly. Practise many 1-10 second random absences with no fanfare or greeting when you leave or arrive. Go through the whole get-ready-to-leave sequence, go out the door and then come back after the specified interval. Try to get in some long sessions where you do tons of them in a row (1 second, 1, 1, 1, 2, 1, 1, 2, 2, 1, 3, 1, 2, 3, 2, 1, 4, 2, 5, 3, 3, 2, 6 etc.). Remember to build up the time only if she is not anxious. Gage this by her demeanor before and after the departure.

I would not suggest crating her although confining her to the kitchen for "damage control" during long absences would be prudent. It would also help set up a safety cue for you insofar as loose-in-house absences would become the safe ones and kitchen absences the anxiety-predicting ones. When you have built her up in exercises to your normal length of absence in real life (which you don't have to do one second at a time, BTW - you increase the increments as the program progresses - it's the beginning part which is slooooow), you simply abandon the kitchen confinement and start leaving her loose in the house.

Adjunct measures such as giving her interesting stuffed Kongs or Activity Balls, increasing exercise and stimulation prior to alone-time and classically conditioning urination and defecation to a verbal cue (so you can empty her) may also be helpful. You can reserve the puzzle toys for the exercise absences to increase the contrast even more between the safe and scary alone-times.

Anti-anxiety medication is often helpful for separation anxiety. It is usually used in conjunction with the behavior therapy outlined above but occasionally milder cases have been resolved with meds alone. After several months of therapy, the dog is gradually weaned off.

Fear of Jumping into the Car

I have an eleven month-old intact male Papillon. He is being trained in Obedience, Conformation and Agility and is usually a very outgoing puppy. However, when we walk to the car he slows down, pulls back and sometimes refuses to approach.

Occasionally he has thrown up in the car. I try to not feed him close to the time we leave so his stomach is empty. I have also tried to make every approach to the car a positive one and he has improved somewhat but still hesitates. When he does jump into the car and into his crate it's very quickly as if he's rushing through something. Once inside the car he's OK. What is this?

There are a couple of likely explanations for your Papillon's reluctance about getting in the car. One is an association with carsickness, and the other is a superstitious fear about loading up. Both would have the symptom of reluctance to approach as well as potentially explaining your other observations.

When dogs are carsick, they presumably feel nauseous which is unpleasant. They don't always throw up so we can't always tell that they're in discomfort. Sometimes they salivate and are restless and sometimes they just pant and look glassy. It's easy to mistake this for a primary car-anxiety. It doesn't take many trials for anxiety to be added, mind you - "oh no, it's that place where my tummy feels bad..." The anxiety is also an aversive, exacerbating the ill feeling, so a vicious cycle is born.

Your dog may no longer feel very carsick but the secondary anxiety that resulted may still be present. If this is the case, your interventions - making positive associations with approach, keeping his stomach empty for travel, and the considerable cumulative effect of so many car rides to enjoyable dog sports - are on the right track and you will probably continue to make gradual gains.

If he is still exhibiting signs of carsickness, try a course of anti-nausea medication to help break the cycle. There are also homeopathic and herbal remedies that it wouldn't hurt to try. Static

149

charge has been implicated in cases of carsickness in both dogs and humans. Cars can drag lines from their undercarriage to the road to dissipate charge. Why not look into this.

The fact that he is fine once in the car but skittish about loading up points to a superstitious fear of some part of the jump-in process. Dogs acquire these fears all the time. For example, if the first time at a baseball game, fireworks go off, the dog subsequently fears kids in baseball uniforms. If, twice in a row, a conformation handler steps on the dog's foot as the rosettes are presented, the dog gets spooky about ribbons. These are considered "superstitious" because there is no logical, rational basis: kids in baseball uniforms don't make big booming noises and rosettes don't hurt feet. The fear remains alive because of the nature of avoidance learning. Subsequent to the chance association, the dog behaves fearfully - balks at the end of the leash or growls at the kids, scrambles away from the rosettes, rushes into the car - and, in his mind, avoids the fearful stimulus. "See how well my behavior works?" He never finds out that the scary thing wouldn't have happened anyway.

Try blocking his avoidance response. Mechanically prevent him from rushing through "something" to get into his crate so he finds out something is nothing. To facilitate this, separate the crate and car elements. Practise going slowly into the car as well as slowly into the crate you use in the car. A halter or plain buckle collar held taut could get you started (keep it taut to avoid his rushing and getting an inadvertent jerk). Do pauses at the "sticky" point (the place he needs to rush through) with treats and praise. The more you hang out at the spot he thinks is dangerous, the more evidence you are giving him that there is nothing scary there. Repeat till he's smooth in that training session. Then go back a day or so later, when the fear response is likely to have bounced back, and do another session, again to the point of relaxed smoothness.

You could also continue as you have been doing, observing closely for gains. Remember to not pressure him. For the sake of more clues, I would try loading him in and out of various crates and other people's vehicles as well. You may even find that this practicing out of context helps you with your own car.

Addison's Disease and Stress Avoidance

My Belgian was diagnosed with Addison's Disease a few weeks ago (it's a shame, she was a great obedience competition dog, well on her way to agility trials, too). She's on the required meds. Of course, these do nothing to stimulate the production of Adrenaline; they only regulate the amount of potassium and sodium in her system. Therefore, I need to watch her for "stressing." All the vet said was "Don't board her." How helpful.

That said, here's my question. What can I do to help her better cope with stressful events (after we identify what they are). Would systematic desensitization be useful in her case?

What an interesting question! There are a few prongs, as I see it, to a possible assault. After identifying as many of her stressors as possible, you can take action. This action will be in the form of treatment, including systematic desensitization and possibly anti-anxiety medication as well as management, which might also include occasional use of anti-anxiety meds. There are "smarter" meds now which do not dope the dog up or inhibit learning. You can also develop a strategy to minimize the likelihood and the potential effects of as-yet-unidentified stressors.

The things she is anxious about should first be ranked according to how severely they stress her. Let's say, hypothetically, that her list looks like this:

High Stress: going to the vet, boarding, sudden loud noises, phobia of revolving signs

Moderate Stress: nail clipping, dogs that come on too strong at the park

Mild Stress: out of sight stays, baths, close proximity of large, strange men

DOGS ARE FROM NEPTUNE

First, examine the list for any you can easily manage. This will save your time and resources for the items you can't work around. Desensitizing dogs to a large variety of things is not feasible for most people. In the High Stress category, two things, revolving signs and boarding, permit the management option of avoidance. You could probably successfully avoid these. I don't know the details of your dog's case but some Addisonian dogs can be pre-medicated with cortisone when you have advance warning of stressful events. It means that things like obedience careers do not always have to be pre-empted. This is another management strategy.

In the case of the vet, you could explore the possibility of housecalls. This is becoming increasingly popular and would at least take care of any routine vaccinations, physical exams or blood work. It would also buy you lots of time to do a series of gradually escalating desensitization visits to the vet clinic to prepare for the possibility of a needed visit or hospitalization. Remember the cornerstone of desensitization, which takes on even greater importance in your case: build on success. Only make the visits harder when she is thoroughly relaxed at the current level. You will make faster progress with many baby steps than with sudden escalations.

Something like a noise phobia - car backfires or T-Storms - is also best treated with desensitization. The most common technique uses a starter pistol at gradually decreasing distance, with food rewards following each shot. It is critical that the initial distance produce no anxiety whatsoever and that the distance be decreased very, very gradually, always monitoring the dog for the smallest sign of worry. For thunderstorms, sound desensitization cassettes are worth trying. In mainstream stores, you can also sometimes find "nature sound" CD's which may include thunderstorms. These are preferable because of the vastly superior sound quality. Play them for long periods at extremely low volume and, when the dog does not respond with any anxiety, gradually raise the volume. Sound-desensitization does not work for all dogs with T-storm phobias. It is thought that the other elements present during storms - air pressure changes, light changes and smells - render the simulation inadequate for these dogs, even if noise is the predominant phobia.

The other way stimulus intensity can be reduced is with anti-anxiety medication. Instead of variables such as distance or volume being manipulated, the dosage is gradually decreased when the dog shows no anxiety. Remember, this is always contingent on relaxation: the dog dictates the pace of progress. Meds can also be combined with the varying of other parameters in severe cases. A combination of meds and CD's is best for a serious thunderstorm problem. Initiate the program at the end of the storm season so that real storms are not sprinkled in.

In the Moderate Stress category, nail clipping could be managed by switching to a filing (or grinding) system. This gives a "fresh start," much like home vet visits do. Also, filing and grinding are procedures which are usually less scary for dogs. Or, you could go with formal desensitization to nail clipping. The idea is the same as with sound desensitization. Start ridiculously easy (picture of nail clippers at 400 yards) and go up a gradual hierarchy, always building on success. Food treats are very helpful here.

Over-gregarious dogs at the park is a management candidate insofar as there are plenty of other exercise options in the universe. The one drawback is the slide in level of socialization if you significantly decrease your dog's number of regular contacts. It could set her up for much greater stress when she does eventually encounter dogs. A bit like trading in a small bubble or two under the rug now for a potentially bigger one later. For this reason, I'd be inclined, with a general social anxiety, to maintain exposure at a tolerable level and pair any contacts with food or other primary reinforcer. If it were just a specific dog or two bullying her, then I would opt for avoidance. I'd also work with the large, strange men in a similar fashion: pair each contact with food rewards to turn that small, gnawing anxiety into "yay! bar open!"

For baths or other low-ish anxiety procedures, do whatever you can to make it tolerable and to soften the blow. None of us do enough blow softening for our dogs. Budget sufficient time so that you can be extremely patient in your handling. Don't ignore details like water temperature, the type of showerhead, non-skid surface, how you move her in and out of the tub, working carefully around eyes, ears and nose and major cookie time afterwards. People who have been in dogs a long time do a lot of these automatically but, when they do miss something, they often don't see the ramifications for the dog. Their handling is so confident and efficient, any rebellion from the dog is squashed. I see this most in the cavalier handling of little dogs but also at dog shows where skillful handlers are able to make dogs stand for judges who frighten them. This is worth considering in a stress-minimization program.

In the case of out-of-sight stays or other training/event type things which stress the dog, the best thing to do, in my opinion, is to simply drop non-essential activities she does not like and find ones she does. At-home training, like clicker training easy tricks, would be a great alternative to competitive obedience for keeping her mind alive. This is not to say that well-executed, aversive-free competitive training with a well-socialized dog wouldn't be an option, if her energy level is up to it. But meeting all of those conditions is not easy.

You can also institute contingency plans for unplanned stressors. Plan a network of emergency dog-sitters, people who understand her situation. Pre-visit their homes until your dog is comfortable there.

Classically condition a calming cue. A certain word or phrase could be paired with massage and soothing talk. Canine bodywork would be an excellent thing for your dog. There are more books and seminars on this than ever before and I think it is wonderful. The power of therapeutic touch is vastly underestimated as a stress reducer. And, finally, there is a world of natural remedies and nutritional wisdom to explore. Anything that would be supportive of overall health can only help.

Severe Separation Anxiety

I have a two and a half year-old Great Pyrenees with extreme separation anxiety. I got Mia when she was five months old from a good home where, although she was loved, I don't think she had any structure or training. The owner, a college student, had to give her up because she barked excessively when left alone.

This barking has continued with me, and has progressively gotten worse. Not only does she bark, but scratches at the doorframe, sometimes to the point of bleeding paws. She'll continue the strange barking/whining/crying sounds for several hours a day.

I have tried every solution I have read about for separation anxiety - toning down arrivals and departures, increasing exercise, behavioral modification exercises. I tried leaving treats for her, but she won't eat while I am gone. I have started her on amitryptalline (Elavil) to try and relieve some of the anxiety, but have not seen much change.

I recently moved, and this made her worse. She panics if I am out of her sight, even if it's for five seconds to put something outside. She immediately flips out, barking and whining. When I come back in, she is crazed at my arrival. She anticipates my leaving for work way before I leave and gets more and more depressed as I get ready. She'll crawl behind my bed, or hide in a corner. She is very needy, follows me around the house, not letting me out of her sight.

Generally, she is a happy dog as long as I am with her. We have taken obedience class together, which she enjoyed immensely. She listens well and we have no other behavior problems. She plays well with other dogs at the local dog park and gets a good amount of exercise.

I feel so frustrated, because I have tried everything I can, working with my vet as well as dog trainers. But I have not seen

DOGS ARE FROM NEPTUNE

any abatement in her behavior; in fact it has gotten worse. I just don't know what else I can do to try to help her.

I know that it is miserable for Mia and life crippling for you that she is so distressed at being left alone. There is good news, though. Separation anxiety is a specific disorder with a very specific and highly effective treatment, systematic desensitization. It is not clear whether the "behavior modification" you refer to was a formal desensitization program or not but I suspect it may have been missing key elements. The track record for systematic desensitization at treating separation anxiety is excellent, provided the instructions are followed to the letter. Severe separation anxiety rarely resolves itself spontaneously, nor does it respond to the informal kinds of measures you have tried, although such things may do the trick in very mild cases.

Your dog has virtually all the defining characteristics of severe separation anxiety: panic attacks with destructiveness and vocalizing when left alone, pre-departure anxiety and depression, intense and protracted "relief" greetings on arrival. She also has a couple of elements in her history that are common to many cases: very long absences early on in life, re-homing and an exacerbation of the problem when the living situation changed. Dogs with separation anxiety are often perfect dogs otherwise: obedient, sociable and pleasant.

To fix separation anxiety, the dog has to experience the situation - being left alone - without the accompanying anxiety. This association is strong in dogs like Mia and often extends to the rituals that she has learned mean departure is imminent, such as you showering, collecting keys, briefcase etc.

Separation anxiety can be extremely specific, to the amazement of owners. Dogs are very good at reading environmental cues that predict events of relevance to them. Many owners of dogs with separation anxiety report that their dogs are wrecks in the early morning Monday to Friday but are fine on weekend mornings. The different pictures predict different scenarios: one a traumatically long absence, one not. The dog is very tuned in to the time of day

156

and what you are doing. Is it a "leaving for work" picture or a "staying" picture?

Many dogs are fine when left in the car but cannot tolerate being left at home. Some dogs are fine if you leave in your slippers with two garbage bags, but panic if you put on work shoes and leave with your purse. Once again, they have learned the pictures associated with lengths of absence that upset them. This learning takes place early on and, once true separation anxiety is up and rolling, the anxiety is self-perpetuating and based solely on the picture.

Therefore, once the problem is in place, it will sometimes seem to contradict strict rules about length of time. If the dog becomes anxious about being left at home but is fine being left in the car, the dog will panic at a five-minute absence when at home but be able to tolerate two hours in the car. This is because the anxiety is already in full swing once the owner is at the door, and usually long before, so, the actual length of time becomes immaterial: it's already a done deal. The "decision" is made.

So, treatment centers on changing the meaning of the picture that formerly kicked off anxiety. This entails doing a series of exercises, "practice absences," of durations the dog can tolerate, and then, very gradually, building up the time. The time is only built up when the dog is exhibiting no anxiety. The barometer for this is the pre- and post-absence behavior of the dog. It is essential to begin the program with exercises that the dog can already tolerate and then build up from there.

In many cases, such as Mia's, the dog will already be anxious by the time the owner steps out the door. A lot of effort must be spent getting the dog to relax in spite of the pre-departure rituals. The key is backtracking to the first thing in your routine that informs Mia that a departure is on the way soon. Be exact about what happens "way before" you leave that kicks off pacing or worrying or depression in Mia. This will be the first target in your desensitization program.

DOGS ARE FROM NEPTUNE

Let's say your morning ritual consists of getting up, walking the dog, eating breakfast, tidying up a bit, showering, drying your hair, dressing, putting on make-up, throwing together a lunch, letting the dog out for a last pee, packing your briefcase, packing a Kong, putting on shoes and coat, feeding the dog, grabbing purse and keys and leaving. And let's say the dog starts looking edgy when you start putting on make-up and is trembling behind the bed by the time you fetch her to take her out. In your training sessions, you will practise, over and over, getting dressed, putting on make-up and then ending the exercise, not leaving. When she is relaxed about the make-up - no pacing, no worried look etc. - start working on the next item in the sequence, making lunch.

In your sessions, do many trials in a row, always monitoring for anxiety level. After several repetitions, any mild existing anxiety should diminish. If it does not, you have not gone back far enough in the sequence. Interestingly, unlike most other training endeavors, alone-desensitization likes long training sessions. You're usually better off, for example, doing one 50-minute session than breaking it up into five 10-minute sessions. And, naturally, the more you work on it, the faster you progress.

Once you've made it to the door (which may take several sessions), start off with very short absences, literally one second. Then come back in, put the keys back, then pick them up and leave again for one second. Do it over and over until it is clearly no big deal for the dog. Then do two seconds. Then three. Then do a few ones again. Then do four. Then do two. Mix it up, always throwing plenty of easy ones in. Only increase time if the dog is not anxious. Think of it as a game you're playing with the dog.

When people consider doing desensitization on their dogs, it seems a discouraging prospect to spend so much time getting the dog over picking up a set of keys or some other component in the departure sequence. Is this always going to be the pace of progress? The answer is no: things get better later. A disproportionate amount of time is required to get the ball rolling in the early stages. You will spend much more time and effort getting the dog to relax about these pre-departure cues than you will adding time increments later on. Once you're out the door and doing absences, progress is much faster. You won't have to always go up in one-second increments either! The point is: don't rush the early work – it's **essential**. This is where you win the dog's trust.

An important component of successful resolution of separation anxiety is the suspension of intolerable absences during the treatment program. While you are working on Mia to fix this, you can't do any real life absences, in other words. As ridiculous as this sounds, it is important. Most people come up with some combination of dog-sitters, day-care, time off work and bringing the dog along. All the absences must be practice absences until the length of practice absence exceeds the length of absences you want to do in real life (and, hence, will feel like practice sessions to the dog). You can only go out for as long as you've achieved in desensitization exercises in other words. Because at the beginning it's usually zero time, you can't go out (note: if suspension of absences is absolutely impossible, a safety cue can sometimes be incorporated to allow the dog to discriminate between safe and unsafe length absences).

This program can be done with the dog on amitryptalline, which may allow for a faster pace. At the end of the program, the dog is gradually weaned off the drug. It takes at least a few weeks to build up in her system so it's not surprising you haven't seen anything from the medication you were prescribed. Also, in a severe case like yours, you ought to combine the meds with the formal program for maximum impact. It would be great if you could find a trainer or behaviorist near you who has experience with SA cases to troubleshoot and support you as you work the program.

DOGS ARE FROM NEPTUNE

SUBJECT INDEX

About the Author

Jean Donaldson is the owner of Renaissance Dog
Training in Montreal, Canada where she lives with
Meggie (l) and Lassie (r). She is also the author of
The Culture Clash and the interactive CD-ROM,
Dogs Behaving Badly!

http://www.lasardogs.com